CU00944498

# Europe and Islam

# Europe and Islam

## *Hichem Djaït*

## Translated by Peter Heinegg

UNIVERSITY OF CALIFORNIA PRESS

BERKELEY • LOS ANGELES • LONDON

University of California Press

Berkeley and Los Angeles, California

University of California Press, Ltd.

London, England

Copyright © 1985 by

The Regents of the University of California

Library of Congress Cataloging in Publication Data

Djaït, Hichem

Europe and Islam

Translation of: L'Europe et l'Islam.

Includes index.

1. Near East—Relations—Europe.

2. Europe—Relations—Near East.

3. Civilization, Islamic.  4. Europe—Civilization.

I. Title.

DS63.2.E8D5213  1985    303.4′824′017671    84-8786

ISBN 0-520-05040-1

Printed in the United States of America

1 2 3 4 5 6 7 8 9

"First published in French under the
title L'Europe et L'Islam. Copyright ©
1978 by Editions du Seuil, Paris. This
translation © 1985 by The Regents of
the University of California."

*To Huguette, Karim, and Nadia,*
*with love*

# Contents

# Introduction

What justification could there be for a comparative study bracketing one concept whose origin is purely geographical with another whose origin is just as purely religious? Even if we take these terms in their current sense and view the realities they stand for in their contemporary context, such a comparison might not be any more intelligible. What, then, is this book about?

Europe today stretches far beyond its boundaries. Intellectually speaking, it serves as the matrix and historical benchmark for America, Australia, even the Soviet Union. In the field of science and technology its discoveries and achievements set the modern standard everywhere. Politically, in contrast, Europe is drawing back, concentrating around its western core, as it tries to build a new identity, restricted and particular, based on specific features that distinguish it from everything which it has projected outside itself or conquered and denied. And so it is a complex entity that can be observed from more than one perspective.

The same is true of Islam. The term itself, used to define a political, cultural, religious, and economic unit, applies only to a single short period, from A.D. 800 to 850. Islam, in fact, has almost never managed to maintain its various constitutive elements at an equal pitch of intensity. At the height of its cohesiveness as a political empire—under the Umayyads— Islam was limited, as a religion, to the victorious Arabs: the great bulk of society was neither converted nor imbued with

Islamic principles or culture. At the height of its cohesiveness as a culture, a faith, a community—from the tenth to the twelfth century—Islam was crumbling politically, as local traditions underwent an increasingly dramatic resurgence. Just as Europe did, Islam left its original center behind to spread both its faith and, to a large extent, the way of life associated with it. This occurred in Indonesia, China, northern India, Asia Minor, the Balkans and, finally, black Africa. As for Iran, which had been closely connected with the development of classical Islamic culture, it broke away from the destiny of Islam before the time of the Safavids, without thereby repudiating the Islamic faith, but rather creating its own version of it.

Nowadays the Arab world is laying claim to the Islamic heritage, and forging the strongest of bonds between that heritage and its historical consciousness. It is playing a part similar to Western Europe's, not just because it was the cradle of Islam (as Europe was of modernity), but because it stands apart as actually different from other "external" or "peripheral" Islamic entities. The Arab world is taking over the historical idea of Islam so as to make it its focal point. Thus the ancient *Umma* is effecting a kind of transferal and shrinkage of all Islamic space into the confines of Arab space, and is becoming charged with an emotionally powerful political-ideological content.

The result is that if Europe, in its commonplace, shrunken present-day form, can find an analogue only in the Arab world, Europe as a historical culture and a great civilization corresponds to Islam as an international community and civilization, or to China, another cultural matrix that spread outward, becoming a model and norm for an immense area. The fact that contemporary Islam is bound together by nothing but faith, and the fact that an originally European mode of civilization, now carried as far afield as New Zealand or the United States, could never claim to be incarnate in any one place, locates both Islam and Europe in history and nowhere else. We must, however, make the basic reservation that we are not dealing with dead cultures but living historical subjects. A philosophy of history a la Spengler would see nothing wrong in lining up antiquity, the ancient East, Islam, Europe, and Amerindian civilization on the same comparative table. Contrariwise, geopolitics, which restricts its purview to the modern scene and has no historical depth-perception, might break the world up into seven, eight, or ten regions or political-economic systems, putting both America and Southeast Asia equally far from Europe.

Although it may be true that no civilization really dies "deep down," the so-called dead civilizations *are* very much dead, both on the level of consciousness and in their singular forms. And the best response to the ahistorical position of geopolitics is not simply to point up all the things that move people in the matter of ideology and culture but to counter the postulate of historical discontinuity by insisting on continuity, to meet arguments for the absolute novelty of modern experience with arguments for the ongoing revival of patterns of action from the past.

This essay labors under one difficulty that has nothing to do with the definition of its terms nor its proposed angle of vision. Islam and Europe are living historical civilizations, with universal intentions; they have known breaks and metamorphoses; they have a center and a periphery. That much can serve as an outline of similarities linking their destinies, and as a justification for the trouble of studying them comparatively. But the European adventure, limited in time to four centuries of creativity, and as questionable as its results may be, has proved decisive and exemplary for all humanity, and will continue to be so. It cannot be compared, we are told, with any other civilization, past or present, except perhaps with that of the Neolithic period. And one cannot dismiss this sort of opinion merely by branding it as Eurocentric, because Europe's accomplishments have de facto exceeded everything ever created by the old civilizations. Even the devotees of non-European historical civilizations never dispute the privileged character of Europe's creations but only their stifling and potentially lethal excess. As opposed to the rational and destructive Euro-American species of humanity, they exalt a humanity that respects nature and loves God, viewed as the European past or its negation.

Consequently, the uniqueness of Europe's destiny would seem to make it incommensurable with (or opposite to) all other societies. Under these conditions how can we justify a comparative study?

Two principal reasons can be offered on this score: first a standard problematic approach, which is already outdated; second, a fundamental assumption, which is less so. Why did Islam—or China—mark time in domains where Europe was off like a shot, in science, analytical thought, technology? Islam is more in question here than China because, if China represents absolute otherness, Islam has a number of things in common with Europe and was even one of the root causes of its rise to eminence. We assume, however, that Europe's conquests are the product of efforts by the whole human race, whether they lived during that time or before: Greco-Roman antiquity, Israel, Islam, China, the Americas. Lévi-Strauss's idea of a "coalition"[1] strikes me as more useful and closer to the truth than the strictly internalist thesis, hitherto the most widely accepted, which sees a basic principle, fecund with possibilities, evolving on its own. Still, the internalist hypothesis ought not to be rejected outright, as some of its explanations remain valid. But the predominant importance of relations with the outside world in Europe's epochal breakthrough should call our attention to the evolution of the other great cultures that nourished it in its fledgling stage, later endured and paid for its expansion and, finally, still survived, to defy the modernity it brought forth.

Muslims have long been fascinated and disoriented by the "success" of Europe, with its industrial and imperial might; and some have been attracted by its humanism and liberalism. One after another, reformers, nationalists, and modernist intellectuals have painted a picture of Europe largely colored by their preoccupation with self-defense, rejection, or mimicry. The emergence of the Muslim world, first on the international political scene and now in the economic sphere; the distance that the Euro-American world has managed, over time, to put between itself and its works, so that it can challenge their rationality; and the increasingly bold synthesis currently taking shape in the heart of Islam between cultural consciousness, rooted in history, and the objective acquisition of the instruments of modernity—all this has rendered the old perceptions of the problem utterly obsolete. Muslim intellectuals can now approach Western civilization as positively as one could wish, not to steal its secrets but to understand it from within, to question it about its essential nature, to explore its contours with both sympathetic commitment and critical detachment. Just when Europe is becoming more tribal, forgetting its history, and getting winded, so to speak, the admirable substance of old Europe is revealing itself to non-Europeans with the freshness of a first encounter.

By the same token, anxious fears that Islam might collapse—as momentarily seemed possible—have been calmed. The idea of cultural pluralism, of equal rights to self-development for all societies, ideas now accepted by open-minded people everywhere, allow Muslims to maintain a certain distance from their identity. The obscure dread of being cut off from their roots in any way has been largely dissipated. Islam is no longer defensively turned in upon itself: neither Westernization nor Marxism appear capable of sapping its cultural foundations. And so historical-critical thought can, by working from within it, get a new grip on the whole situation. The Islamic intelligentsia can look at normative Islam from a certain remove, demythologizing its past without the nervous rigidity of self-accusation. A split is opening up—though it ought to be more pronounced—in the self's attachment to itself, which is the precondition for attaining truth.

Europe has scarcely begun to leave off contemplating itself as the center of the world, the axis of civilization, the goal of history. Having been challenged and relativized, it is now setting about the task of thinking over its origins. This auto-reflection, first noticeable in the area of politics, is symptomatic of doubt and disarray. It could be the prelude to a desperate kind of self-glorification. In any case, Europe can no longer ignore the world outside or the modesty of its origins. But neither can Islam go on ignoring what was Europe's inner drive, its substance and purpose nor can it continue to perceive itself in monolithic and mythical terms. We are headed nowadays toward an unprecedented confrontation of civilizations. The interests as well as inertial forces that massed the great bodies of humanity around their particular axes are going to have recourse both to modern ideological constructs and to ancient crystallized patterns. The more unified the world gets, the greater the temptation to seek differentiation, internal structure, and articulation by clustering around one dominant pole or another. Once this happens it becomes perfectly apparent that a certain generation of individuals from "non-Europe" (to borrow Laroui's expression) must act as mediators.

They have to bring to their world the triumphs not of technology but of critical intelligence, informed by history and philosophy. They do not necessarily, not at first anyway, have to put European categories of rationality on trial. Their role is rather to expose the whole range of European experience, in depth, to other norms, other values, and perhaps other categories. This is the way to hammer out a universal that will not be utopian nor destructive but the outcome of creative synthesis.

# PART I
# IN ANOTHER'S EYES

# 1

# From the Medieval Vision to Modern Visions

*The Christian Orient and Islam*

It is clear that Jewish hostility to Muhammad's preaching at Medina grew out of a feeling of contempt fed by the awareness of religious superiority vis-à-vis something that might be taken for a counterfeit biblical tradition. But this superiority was also based on an ancient heritage of book learning, on national and cultural pride. The Jews had declined to accept Jesus, a figure who developed within the context of Judaism, and they did the same with Muhammad, who was totally foreign to it. If the Christians of Najran behaved in a more reserved and less combative fashion, it was doubtless because, although they were more Arabian than the Jews, they were far removed from the fierce struggles for power in Medina. Hence we find a certain fundamental sympathy for Christianity in the Qur'an and a freedom from the passion directed at the Jewish population of Medina, viewed as a censor and monitor, as well as a model.

Once the Jewish community of Medina was subdued, the Arab conquest would have to deal primarily with Christians. It has been said again and again that Monophysite Christians in

9

the East were eager to bow beneath the political yoke of the
conquering Arabs because they hoped to get more tolerant
treatment at their hands. This notion is quite correct, provided
one qualifies it somewhat. The Arab conquest, after all, must
have seemed like a destructive hurricane, a painful catastrophe.
We hardly know anything about what sort of intellectual reactions Christians first had to Islam. Some chronicles from the
seventh century suggest a rather favorable response. Sebeos,
for example, accepts the Abrahamic roots of Islam and stops just
short of recognizing a certain authenticity in Muhammad's
prophetic writings. [1] But Abu Qurra, who wrote in the middle of
the eighth century, displays only a crude knowledge of Islamic
doctrine, and the chapter on Islam in John Damascene's *De
heresibus*, which attempts to liken the new religion to Arianism,
seems actually to be a ninth-century interpolation. [2]

During the Umayyad epoch, Christianity, both in Byzantium and the Middle East, obviously had a much better theological arsenal at its command than did Islam, whose theology
was almost nonexistent then and which came about only as a
counterthrust to attacks by Christian authors, from whom they
borrowed their concepts and methods. [3] The Islamic *Kalam* came
out of a Syrian or Syro-Mesopotamian environment and an
atmosphere of theological dispute with the original inhabitants.
Still, the crucial fact here is that the Christian East, though much
more advanced than the West, was now living as the ward of a
state that was certainly tolerant but not indifferent, since it
already had its own religion.

Owing to the fact that eastern Christianity lost its political
voice and power, the evolution of its attitude toward Islam has
no relevance to a study aimed at the confrontation between
civilizations. As time went on, however, political Christianity
came to identify itself with the European West (except for Byzantium which, hindsight tells us, had no future), a process that
culminated in the Crusades. Christendom, that purely Western
phenomenon, was not merely a religious community. It wanted
to be a political body, and to a great extent it was. It gave birth to
modern Europe, which is saying a good deal, but this means that

the essential factor here was its autonomy, not its (initially crude) level of culture. And this autonomy had no meaning in the Middle Ages apart from Europe's relationship to Islam.

## The West: Hostility and Controversy

Between the eighth and the tenth century, the Christian West felt in its body and soul the final thrusts of the Arab conquest, which was getting its second wind about that time. Even though the waves of the Saracen assault only lapped its edges, in Spain, southern Italy, and southern France, the Christian world had only known intervals of peace for centuries, and now it was being threatened again. Clearly it had no choice, in the beginning, but to liken these incessant attacks, launched in the name of a well-organized imperial state, to the other barbarian, anarchic invasions it had been subjected to earlier. This led to some confused thinking, which persists even today, so that Marc Bloch speaks of the "lairs" of the Arabs, of their "profitable raids," and describes le Freinet as "the most dangerous brigands' nest of all."[4]

This original experience of Arab aggression served the medieval Western mind as the source for the basic affective element in its thinking about Islam, which was essentially steeped in hostility. But during the high Middle Ages the West was trapped wihin its own narrow horizon and could not produce a coherent and reasonably informed view of Islam. Only Spain, in the ninth century, thought it discerned in Muhammad the features of the Antichrist, but later dropped this idea, only to return to it toward the end of the *reconquista*.[5] Carolingian tradition was unaware of such notions or at any rate did not go along with them, and we know that in other respects both empires were on good terms.

Like the intellectual awakening in Ireland, the Carolingian renaissance was not concerned with Islam. But it was a different story when medieval culture solidified and Christian Europe flung itself upon the outside world in the Crusades.

Here we have to distinguish popular conceptions of Islam from those of Scholasticism. The first drew upon the Crusades, the second upon the Islamic-Christian confrontation in Spain. One addresses the imagination, the other looks to reason. In popular literature, Muslims were pagans and Muhammad was a magician, the depraved ruler of a depraved people. The *Chanson de Roland*, blending epic themes and extravagant fancy, presents the Saracens as idolatrous worshipers of Tervagaunt. The learned view of Islam, in contrast, contained some genuine information. Thanks to the *Corpus Cluniense* (1143) and to Ketton's translation of the Qur'an, scholastic controversialists drank, as it were, from the source.[6] Peter the Venerable, Mark of Toledo, Ricoldo, Raymond Martin, Jacques de Vitry, and later Raymond Lully and Nicholas of Cusa were perfectly familiar with the doctrines of Islam. No doubt we must differentiate anti-Islamic controversy from the influence of Islamic philosophy on the great scholastic writers. But to some degree controversy is a form of defense, and the intellectuals engaged in polemics were in a way open-minded individuals who felt ill at ease with their own provincialism. Saint Bernard was infinitely more closed off to the outside world than Peter the Venerable. Arrogance and self-deception did not necessarily preclude interest or, perhaps, even fascination concerning the enemy.

Because of its philosophy and scientific advances, Islam was implicitly recognized as a key contributor to the history of thought. But while acknowledged on one hand, it was denied, on the other, as a religion and ethical system—though all its aspects were taken into consideration. Thus the West dissociated the achievement of Arab thinkers from its judgment on the value of Islam.

This position was worked out in the twelfth century, broadened and specified in the thirteenth and fourteenth, and survived practically unchanged until the eighteenth century. Some elements of it lasted up to the colonial era.[7] Its point of departure was a deep anger at the Prophet for having blocked humanity's evolution toward universal Christianity by his "false prophecy." Men as unlike one another as Raymond Martin, Ricoldo, Mark of Toledo, or Roger Bacon seem to have been incapable of doubting that Muhammad was a false prophet, an impostor, and a hypocrite. His message was merely a human message, dictated by the dark schemes of personal, worldly motives; and the Qur'an was nothing but a collection of fables borrowed from the Bible and warped by the author. The Prophet's crime was not only that he exploited the credulity of the masses but that he was throughout his life the prime example of the sensualism, violence, and immorality with which he stamped the nations who followed him.

As excessive as these judgments may be, they arose from the possibility, which was not initially rejected, of admitting Islam into the body of Christian truth. Christian apologists simply wished to show that Islam was in error according to the canons of the Church, to deny the Prophet's claim to be a real prophet, and to prove that the word of God was the word of God. From this standpoint, therefore, Allah is God—and not the barbarous and specifically Arab god of modern social science—but he did not speak to Muhammad. This was not, in other words, the a priori, across the board rejection that forms the background of all modern assessments of Islam, but an a posteriori rejection of a real, but unrealized, possibility. It was actually a quarrel raging within the walls of a single system.

Over the centuries Christian tradition came to look upon Islam as a disturbing, upstart movement that awakened such bitter passion precisely because it laid claim to the same territory as Christianity. Whatever its triumphs, it was no more than a badly armed, primitive newcomer, simplistic on the whole, and with only rudimentary doctrine. Its success in the world was no evidence of its truth, but a challenge to the truth and a permanent divine scandal, insofar as God, in his impenetrable wisdom, had armed, trained, and assured the victory of evil and lies.

Along with this went a vision of the Muslim soul, which sprang from the same conditions that fostered pseudoproph-

ecy. The behavior of the Muslim prophet was the antithesis of
saintly behavior, the latter being founded on instinctual repres-
sion. In its whole outlook, especially its conception of paradise,
Islam was carnal and materialistic. Its laws and institutions only
fed that lethal germ that infected its lifeblood. If the Islamic
notion of paradise betrayed the fact that here was a religion
devoid of spirituality, smothered in images of future delight,
and smelling strongly of paganism, the life of the Prophet in
turn proclaimed the inauthenticity of his faith. One may wonder
whether the sexual obsession that racked this little world of
celibate European intellectuals did not play some part in their
horror-stricken fascination with Islam, which they supposed to
be a religion of sex, licentiousness, and the exuberant savagery
of animal instinct.

Together with the message of the Qur'an and the life of the
Prophet, the teachings and social institutions of Islam, in the
eyes of medieval Christians, confirmed the idea of Muslim
sensuality. Polygamy was naturally highlighted and denounced
as a pleasure that intoxicated its practitioners, making them
soft, enervated, and effeminate.[8] Woman was considered a servant, not a companion, *serva non socia*, which ran counter to the
Christian view. Finally, the Qur'an says that homosexuality is
permitted in paradise; apropos of that, William of Auvergne
remarks that polygamy failed to wipe out homosexuality, as
might have been expected.[9] In a word, Islamic society was perceived, morally speaking, as a society that did not rate "chastity
as one of the public virtues." Islam was naively presented as
favoring sexual license, as the domain of untrammeled animal-
ity; and, more naively still, this libertinage was traced back to a
cult of sensuality inaugurated by the Prophet.[10]

Alongside sexuality, a second theme elaborated by the
medieval West was that of aggression, force, and violence. "The
use of force," Daniel tells us, "was almost universally considered as a major constitutive characteristic of Islamic religion
and an evident sign of error."[11] This Muslim violence, so deeply
and unanimously resented, was at once the projection of the

West's own violence onto Islam, the influx of ancient terrors into the collective unconscious, and the here-and-now, objective (though exaggerated) apprehension of a real violence. Authors who expressed their thoughts in rational discourse drew a contrast between Christianity, which had been propagated by conversion and the exemplary sufferings of the Apostles, and Islam, which had divided the world into *Dar al-Islam* and *Dar al-Harb* with all the ideology and mystique of violent domination implied by that distinction. Finally, turning from the general topic of the spirit of a people or a religion to the particular acts that manifest and bear witness to it, these writers speak about the law of force imposed by the Prophet upon his followers so that he could impose upon the world, about the persecution of the Church, the profanation of transforming God's churches into mosques, or "synagogues of Satan," and the dismembering of Christendom by the Arab invasion. Last of all, they argued that Islam would not engage in rational debate, in the *disputatio* or, as we would say, it resisted conversion campaigns by apologists for Christianity.

The very existence of Islam, which was autonomous but nonetheless invoked a common tradition, thus appeared as a challenge to Christian totalitarianism, with its distinctive awareness of ancient legitimacy and its unfamiliarity with religious pluralism. The unity of the medieval West was nurtured by the humus of Roman culture, whereas Islam had to come to terms with a multireligious society in a gradual process of absorption.

What interest does the medieval vision have today? It adds nothing to our knowledge of Islam, but it does tell us a bit about the mentality of certain groups of intellectuals in the Middle Ages. It was obviously a polemical vision, but for that very reason it exhibits a sense of inferiority. Every question about the other masks an obsession with the other. And if classical Islam was indifferent toward the West, that was not due to a lack of curiosity on its part, but because it had nothing to gain from the West and so ignored it. Still, those medieval prejudices crept so deeply into the collective unconscious of the West that one fears they may never be uprooted.


## MODERN EUROPE AND ITS IMAGE OF ISLAM

As Christendom gave way to Europe, and Christianity progressively lost its ideological monopoly, Islam, starting about the sixteenth century, ceased to be thought of as the primordial enemy or the serpent in the bosom. In spite of this development, the core of medieval notions about Islam, though cut off from its source, had a life of its own and continually threatened to burst out afresh whenever any conflict arose between the two worlds.

It was evident that, overshadowing this persistence, a major break had occurred within the European mind. But there was more than one modern Europe. There was the Europe that grew out of the Renaissance and the Reformation, out of Enlightenment Europe, and post-1850 imperialist Europe. And at the heart of each of these Europes various circles met and overlapped, thereby creating different viewpoints: that of the politician, the priest, the merchant, the intellectual, the sahib.

In the sixteenth and seventeenth centuries the religious consciousness of the West was no longer at war with Islam. But it never managed to transcend its dogmatic past and continued to fire away at the truth of Muhammad's prophecy. This is the context one must keep in mind when reading the section devoted to the Prophet in the *Pensées*: Pascal's ideas are a vestige of the old medieval disputes.[12] The Church and its theologians more commonly ignored Islam, even if they were familiar with Muslims. Their sense of superiority in possessing the truth was matched by an awareness of political and cultural supremacy. Things were finally right with the world since military power and civilization now coincided with the truth. And Islam returned to the status of barbarism, in that it was expelled from the common sphere where medieval tradition could come to grips with it, if only to prove it wrong. It had ceased to be viewed as a theological adversary—a force that one controverted, yet for that very reason had to take seriously—but as a primitive religion which did not belong in humanity's spiritual mainstream. Throughout the modern period, Christianity would thus represent the most powerful source of Western hostility to Islam.

The profane world took a different tack, increasingly facing up to social reality as time passed. Secular thought, in the realms of both intellectual speculation and practical politics, freed itself from the pressure of Christian beliefs and opened itself to a new *Weltanschauung*. Accordingly it developed a profound sense of Islam as an integral and important part of human life.

On the political level, Islam was identified with the Ottoman Empire. The Arabs were vanishing from the European horizon while Turkish Islam was finding a place there. This led to relations of a largely secularized nature, governed primarily by the rationale of diplomacy. Of course, there was the Holy League and Pius V's efforts against the Turks, but was Lepanto a battle between religions or between political powers? And when the Spanish captured Grenada in 1492, after one of history's great rebellions over national identity, the issue was as much a conflict of political loyalties as a confrontation between civilizations. And compared with the monolithic Turkish Empire it was pitted against, Europe still seemed fragile.

Western intellectuals began to take a broader and more diversified view of Islam, the Orient, and the Muslim soul. Their approach to these subjects became more direct and more serene. They now looked upon the Orient (framed in essentially Turco-Persian terms) as a civilization. Popular thinking successively conjured up images of a splendid Orient, full of marvels, of the cruel, lascivious Oriental, of the primitive, violent Berber, and all this capped by a vision of Islam: fanatically religious, aggressive, simpleminded. Whereas uneducated people thought of the Orient as somehow both droll and frightening, the intellectual elite was concerned only with a kind of "serious" Islam and Orient, freed of particularism.

Of course, the more Europe refined its cultural instruments, the more it took itself to be the center of the world. And the more it drew itself up to look out over the rest of the world, the more it found the view picturesque. This attitude might have turned into contempt, but the eighteenth century's enthusiasm, optimism, and universalism prevented that. Insofar as it postulates a common human nature, universalism assumes that all cultures have an equal potential for developing it. This changes universalism into relativism.

Apart from the Orientalists, who were fixated on "cultural essentialism"[13] and looked to the past, who conferred a privileged status dogmatically upon classical Greco-Roman culture and implicitly upon contemporary Western society, the great centers of eighteenth-century Europe all showed a persistent desire to understand Islam. One need merely cite Boulainvilliers and Goethe, to a certain extent Voltaire and Montesquieu, and even Napoleon, to be convinced of this.

How much did the eighteenth century owe its generosity to the fact that it was not infected by a gangrenous will to domination? We might ask whether there wasn't a fundamental break between the eighteenth century and the nineteenth, with its imperialism, its industry, and its bourgeoisie; whether with the de facto universalization of the nineteenth century the era of universalism as an ideal goal did not come to a close. That could explain the way colonized peoples seeking to combat triumphalist, trivial Europe invoked the ideas of the eighteenth century, which had been paradoxically disseminated by the nineteenth as if to negate itself.

For in the second half of that expansionist century the phenomenon that shaped and conditioned Europe's whole outlook was imperialism. Supercilious ethnocentrism justified foreign domination, which in turn fueled ethnocentrism. The entire non-European world was devalued, stripped of its historical dignity, and relegated to the field of ethnology. To the degree that Islam maintained a posture of latent aggressiveness, it was denounced as a vile den of fanatics, while pan-Islamism was accused of being a plot against Europe. Europe expropriated lofty insights from the eighteenth century to do some very down-to-earth business, and it went back to the polemic arsenal of the Middle Ages in order to discredit those it had subdued. Nothing could be more eclectic than imperialism: depending on the situation, it identified itself indiscriminately with the most contradictory causes. Thus it was that the radical French Jacobins leaned on the Church abroad though they fought it at home, and Orientalism used first Christianity and then secular humanism as a stick to beat Islam. Moreover, imperial Europe found its ultimate justification in the idea of a civilizing or liberating mission—something it picked up from the rubble of the eighteenth century which, true to its prosaic and particularist form, it rejected both in spirit and in deed.

Even the twentieth-century liberal critique of colonialism and imperialism has failed to reach the level of disinterested-ness attained by the eighteenth. Perhaps it was driven by the dialectic of history to deny Europe's superiority in the name of a certain idea of Europe. Western intellectuals fall into ethno-centrism even when they think they are questioning it, since they presume that they alone are qualified to define universal values. But this is an unformulated, largely unconscious ethno-centrism, and it has prompted a struggle that, when all is said and done, challenges Western domination.

Eurocentrism crops up more noticeably in groups with a strong ideological commitment, among Christians, whether of the right or left, and Marxists. Both these groups may profess sympathy for the Muslim world, but from different viewpoints. The Christian is drawn to Islamic spirituality, but he prefers to have for his interlocutor a modernist on the verge of unbelief. The Marxist is blind to everything in Islam except its purely modern dimensions, and so he chooses to ignore its inner cul-tural life, which is bound up with the past. The Christian humanist prizes individuation, the Marxist prizes universality —in its only valid form, namely Marxism. Perhaps the man most free of Eurocentrism is the one who worships at no ideological shrine. The less he knows *of* Islam or *about* Islam, the greater his chances of observing it with sympathy if not objectivity. The less he sees through it, the more he grasps it. It was Europe that invented the cultural notion of Islam as a totality. Why should it still refer to that concept now that the Muslim world is politically shattered and Islam itself has been reduced to functioning only as a religion? Europe no longer debates with Islam, but there is an ongoing argument in the minds of Europeans between themselves and the world, and in the minds of Muslims between themselves and "their" Europe.

# 2

# French Intellectuals and Islam

The French intellectual, that leading actor on the stage of European cultural history, began to emerge at about the end of the seventeenth and the beginning of the eighteenth century. He proved to be a writer rather than a scholar, an independent thinker, detached from the machinery of state power, a social critic, conscious of his responsibility and perhaps, as Bernanos said, imbued with the conviction of the superiority of *l'esprit*. He lacked the depth of the Germanic *Wissenschaftler*, but he was skilled in the arts of communication. From Voltaire to Sartre he was always a fighter. I have chosen three manifestations of the type: the eighteenth-century *philosophe*, the Romantic traveler, the *engagé* intellectual of the 1950s.

### ENLIGHTENMENT *Philosophes*: VOLTAIRE AND VOLNEY

Let us start by examining the case of Voltaire, who took a fairly close look at Islam, especially at its religious aspects.[1] In the first phase, with *Mohammed and Fanaticism*, Voltaire's judgment of Islam, which he equated with the Prophet's mission, was disparaging, even hostile. Later, with the *Essai sur les moeurs*, his tone became more restrained and nuanced, but the overall judgment remained harsh. Of course, in the first phase, the object of his attacks on Islam was religion in general and official Christianity in particular. But it is important to note that he fastered on Islam as a symbol of fanaticism, antihumanism,

21

and the will to power. Though part of a larger design, the critical shafts fired at Islam and its Prophet *were* aimed specifically at them and reveal an unmistakable antipathy.[2] Contrary to what Daniel maintains, this was not the resurgence of a medieval prejudice, but a new evaluation of Islam as a religious force and of the broad vision that inspired it.

This appraisal underwent some notable alterations under the influence of the writings of Boulainvilliers. The *Essai sur les moeurs* attempts to analyze the constitutive features of Islam within the framework of the history of religion. This perspective allows Voltaire to distinguish between the Prophet's own contribution and the later evolution of the Islamic religious system. For Voltaire, Muhammad remains a man who played upon the credulity of his fellows and imposed his message by brute force.

Islam, however, was seen as moving toward greater tolerance and as approximating, thanks to its loose sexual standards, something like a system of natural religion. Jesus was good, but Christians became intolerant, whereas Muslims were tolerant despite their evil prophet. Positive development in one case, negative in another: this was Voltaire's way of harmonizing his many contradictory ideas on the subject, of reconciling his prejudices with his reason.

This dissociation of the Prophet from historical Islam, as it appeared in the pages of *L'Essai sur les moeurs*, was a new and important concept. Up till then, Islam had been identified with its founder and swallowed up by him. And if one followed up the implications of the perennial theme of Muhammad's imposture, one might say that he had been, by a monstrous paradox, the only Muslim without real faith, since he would have known that he was an impostor.[3] It is nonetheless clear that even for the later Voltaire the Prophet had somehow laid the groundwork for the Islamic personality.

Those character traits, and the intense discomfort they caused, can be found in a thinker as remote from Christianity as possible, Edward Gibbon. Gibbon took care not to reach any final conclusions, wavering between Muhammad the enthusiast and Muhammad the impostor.[4] Still he surmised the complexity of the man and his evolution over time, thereby glimpsing an idea beloved of nineteenth-century Islamologists: the supposed split between the Meccan and Medinan periods. The eighteenth-century approach to the problem of Islam is characterized, apart from judgments on its religious and prophetic core, by an interest in the current state of Islamic society and a quest for the causes of its decline. In general that decline was perceived as both the breakdown of a civilization and as an example of political decay, although the Ottoman Empire was still powerful.

In Montesquieu, Voltaire, and Volney, whom I shall discuss in some detail, the idea emerges that the backwardness of Islamic society can be explained by the failure of its government, that is, of its political institutions, as well as by the structure of its religion.[5] Turkish despotism was held responsible for this state of affairs, which was *ipso facto* defined as temporary. Voltaire, for example, crisply suggests that those societies might get on their feet again, "owing to the profound and universal human vocation to attain a better constitution, a better lot in life, and a higher level of culture," if they managed to get better governments and more rational and equitable laws.[6] We may notice that the secular thought of the Enlightenment makes optimistic projections about the future, but that certain elements in its treatment of Islam, such as religion or temperament (see Montesquieu's theory of climates), refer to permanent, basic conditions—which casts a veil of ambiguity over a vision that at first seemed clear.

Volney (1757–1820) was one of the major ideologues of his day. On the eve of the Revolution he set out on a long journey to the Orient, which resulted in his *Description of Egypt and Syria*. He later made use of this experience to flesh out his magnum opus, *Les Ruines*. In this second book, Volney makes a number of sweeping estimates of Islam and its founder. One thing he discusses is violence: "Mohammed succeeded in building a political and theological empire at the expense of those of Moses and of Jesus' vicars."[7] Or, in a scene where he has an imam speaking about "the law of Mohammed": "God has established

Mohammed as his minister on earth; he has handed over the
world to him to subdue with the saber those who refuse to
believe in his law."[8] Volney denounces the "apostle of a merci-
ful God who preaches nothing but murder and carnage," the
spirit of intolerance and exclusiveness that "shocks every notion of justice." The Prophet is described (by Christian theologians) as an ambitious man who put religion to work for "his
worldly aims and his plans of dominion," while the Qur'an was
"a tissue of vague, contradictory declamations, of ridiculous,
dangerous precepts."[9] Though he acknowledges the irrational
component of Christianity, Volney makes a point of contrasting
"its gentle, compassionate morality and its wholly spiritual
affections" with Islam, which he faults for—astonishingly
enough—its contempt of science, its pandering to greed and
other base instincts (by threatening cowards with hell and
promising paradise to the brave), in a word its utterly crude
morality, which bears the mark of the barbarism it grew out of.
But this barbarism, instead of evincing behavior in accordance
with its purely active, amoral nature, erected itself into a religious system, into the Word of God and an obsessive model.

These objections have continued to be a frightening and
haunting part of Western thinking about Islam since the Middle
Ages. Here, though, we might seem to have something more
than just a reprise of old familiar themes. Volney, remember,
was not a Christian, was in fact a staunch anti-Catholic. He had
an open mind and good eyes, he observed and learned. But
there is a wide gap separating observation, however perspica-
cious, of a country's customs and economic life from intimate,
sympathetic appreciation and comprehension of a religious system with its merits and flaws. Volney lacked genuine historical
and philological knowledge of Islam. But while he was bound to
borrow—given his inability to explore it in depth—various
medieval *topoi*, which had become both a living tradition and an
oppressive heritage for all intellectuals, he at least tested them
against his experience and made them his own.

In a very important passage of his *Travels in Egypt and Syria*
dealing with the political condition of Syria, Volney gives a

straightforward presentation of his thoughts on the spirit of Islam and its role in the world.[10] It deserves to be quoted at length:

> So far from helping to remedy the abuses of government, the spirit of Islamism, one might say, is their original source. To be convinced of this, simply examine the book which is the repository of that spirit. . . . Anyone who reads the Koran will be forced to admit that it has no idea either of man's duties in society or of the formation of the body politic or of the principles of the art of governance; in brief, it says nothing about what constitutes a legislative code. The only laws it contains can be reduced to four or five ordonnances concerning polygamy, divorce, slavery, and the inheritance rights of close relatives. . . . If amidst the babel of this perpetual delirium any grand design or coherent meaning ever breaks through, it speaks with the voice of an obstinate, impassioned fanaticism. The ear rings with words like *the impious ones, infidels, enemies of God and the Prophet, zeal for God and the Prophet.* . . . There you have the spirit of the Koran! . . . The inevitable consequence of all this is to set up the most absolute despotism in the person of the ruler through the blindest self-sacrifice on the part of his followers. And this indeed was Muhammad's goal. He wanted, not to enlighten but to reign. He sought, not disciples but subjects. Of all the men who have dared to give laws to nations none, assuredly, was ever more ignorant than Muhammad. Of all the absurd creations of the human mind none is more wretched than his book. The history of Asia over the past 1200 years can attest to this, for should one wish to pass from a specific topic to general considerations, it would be easy to prove that the troubles of the State and the ignorance of the people in that part of the world are more or less directly traceable to the Koran and its morality.

The Muhammad described here is diametrically opposed to the lawgiver of the *Aufklärung*, and Volney's diatribe betrays both the presence of received ideas and a biased reading of the

Qur'an. His central intuition (which we also find in Montesquieu and Voltaire) is that social and political institutions are
the cause of the decadence of Oriental society. And those institutions grow right out of the spirit of Islamic religion, which
contains the seed of despotism. Volney even tends to link the
decadence of the Orient to the arrival of Islam, contrasting the
pre-Islamic and post-Islamic Middle East. The only exception he
is willing to make, and a grudging, contradictory one at that, is
for the "al-Ma'mûn Arabs," an evanescent race that ultimately
disappeared.

Volney criticizes a society by criticizing the state, which
leads in turn to a critique of its religion: a concatenation that
would later enjoy a certain vogue. One could hardly expect an
ideologue of his day (who was, besides, rather badly informed)
to penetrate the very essence of Islam. But it is striking that
Volney wished to limit the Qur'an to a legislative code and the
spirit of Islam to mere obedience.

It is necessary, then, to distinguish Volney's judgments
about Islam, which are mediocre, from his reports and reflections on the Arab Near East in the late eighteenth century,
which are extremely valuable. It might be interesting to look at
an example of the latter. There is a fascinating passage in the
*Travels* that deals with "the customs and character of the inhabitants of Syria."[11] It is a systematic account, carefully worked
out yet at the same time down to earth because it is based on
observation as critical as it is sympathetic.

To be sure, the author does not go so far as to discuss the
abstract concept of personality; but his work surpasses the scattered pseudoethnological notes of many of the travelers who
preceded him. Volney also repudiates most of the clichés about
the Oriental mind. He is not satisfied with describing, he explains, and in so doing he rises to a respectable level of coherent
generalization. Thus from the very start he rejects Montesquieu's theory of climates, presenting a tightly argued case from
history and sociology. The notion of Asiatic indolence is, he
maintains, a false one; and in any case it was never continually
valid since in olden times fiercely energetic conquerors imposed

their law on the East, and since everywhere in the world we can observe the ebbs and flows of a society's, and even an individual's, energy, with moments of hyperactivity and moments of inertia, according to circumstances. And at this point Volney's comparative historiography generates two ideas of paramount importance. The first, rather offhandedly introduced, is the law of the challenge posed by the environment, which Toynbee later amplified and systematized. The second one, much closer to the heart of his thought, anticipates Kardiner's findings on the connection between institutions and personality structures. He writes,

> Upon reflection it seems that the nature of the land has a real influence on behavior. It appears that in society, as in the wild, a country where the means of subsistence are somewhat hard to come by will have more active and industrious inhabitants than a country where nature is lavish with her gifts—there the people will be inactive and sluggish. . . . This would suggest the principle that people have a tendency to indolence *not* insofar as they live in warm countries but insofar as they live in rich countries; . . . but . . . we must acknowledge that there are more inclusive and significant factors here than the nature of the land, namely those social institutions called *government* and *religion*. These are what actually determine the activity or inertia of individuals and nations; and, depending upon whether they broaden or narrow the range of human needs (whether natural or redundant), extend or contract the scope of man's activities.

The frame of reference shaping these remarks owes far more to political science (concentrating on relations between the state and society) than to social psychology, and it is still more remote from anything resembling a psychoanalytically oriented sociology. The psychological observations that Volney does make, based on patterns of behavior and empirically perceptible character traits, are hesitant in differentiating the various human types and social strata. Indolence and passivity are taken to be fundamental aspects of life, and Volney builds his theories on them. Ottoman tyranny, with its lust for plunder and its dispiriting policies, crushes productive effort before it can get started, thereby forming the character of Turkish subjects and inclining them to indolence. This situation is especially conspicuous among the well-to-do and merchant classes, because "it is remarkable that when these people set to work, they display a liveliness and an intensity almost unknown among us."

Despite all these regressions, thousands of years of history lie deep in the soul of the Oriental. He is gentle, engaging, human, generous. He "has greater delicacy and openness, both in thought and manners" than even the Frenchman, "as if, having been civilized long before us, the Asians still bore the marks of their earliest education." And among Orientals one can always tell the Muslim by his steadiness in the face of life's storms, by his courage, serenity, and rectitude, whereas the craftiness and instability of Greek Christians come from their state of subjection, which obliges them to meet the violence of their world with cunning.

Though flawed by prejudice and naivete, Volney's study of sexuality has a certain relevance. He seems to think that Islamic civilization knows nothing of love, in that it robs the sexual instinct of all the accessory elements that create love's charm. Lovers, when there are any, can taste only a fugitive and hunted happiness, as if they were criminals—whence the necessity of extreme discretion. Polygamous marriage is a degrading hell. It constitutes, in a way, a fantastic victory of man's ego over the ruins of the life of another (i.e., his wives). But most of the time the satiety he experience makes him lose all desire, and constant household quarrels force him into the role of the flattered and detested tyrant. We have here a distinctly somber image of urban bourgeois society, where husbands and wives are alienated from one another, where authentic contact is broken off, where virtue itself is continually set at nought.

In Voltaire, Montesquieu, and Volney we find neither the sympathy of Boulainvilliers, nor mystical enthusiasm, but politics, character analysis, history of religion and institutions, all of which culminate in either an internal critique of the West or a comparative vision of various civilizations. The West is undoubtedly standing over the world and looking down, but the less direct that look, the more objective it is. The more caught up in concrete details, the harsher it is. That is why the travelers of the Romantic era are ultimately more prosaic than the philosophes, as they glide from abstract thoughts to images, from a sense of history's universality to a sense of its particularity. In any case it is obvious that the Romantics wanted to visit the East for the aesthetic dividends to be gotten there.

## SOME ROMANTIC TRAVELERS

If I may venture a parallel between Chateaubriand and Lamartine, I would suggest that one was forever haunted by the medieval Christian past, with its grandeur, its hatreds, and its fantasms, whereas the other turned his eyes toward a universal future in which the fate of God and man would be played out. Both writers are alike in that they paint portraits (drawn vigorously and pitilessly in the first case, seriously and delicately in the second) of the Islamic character, whose traits they, like their predecessors, explain by going back to the spirit and primal influence of religion. For Chateaubriand, cruelty, despotism, servility, and fanaticism come together in those nations that, by the very structure of their history, "belong essentially to the sword." This history, as he sees it, was barbarous; it negated civilization and justified that awe-inspiring movement, the Crusades. It would be hard to imagine a more Manichaean attitude than Chateaubriand's in the *Itinerary from Paris to Jerusalem*. With incomparable vehemence and stylistic brilliance he evokes all the passions of the medieval period, reaffirming it as he glories in the splendors of a brutal and exclusive "we," echoing, continuing, and reappropriating the Middle Ages as the core of a great tradition and a moment of truth in history.[12]

Lamartine addresses these problems from a different angle, because he was involved in a search for his own identity and

because Western Christian tradition of the narrowest ethno-
centric sort was foreign to him. We see in Lamartine the usual
attempt to summarize the Muslim character, to which, however, he responds appreciatively, stressing pity, charity, fatal-
istic resignation, tolerance (accompanied by fanaticism), along
with a sense of honor and poetic feeling. The author poses his
subjects effectively, and describes vivid scenes in which Muslims, at once real and fictitious, noble, gentle, resigned, quiet,
and serene, touched his heart. But are his Wahhabi shaykh and
Turkish governor individuals in their own right or play-actors?
This is a forceful reminder of how hard it is for the inner essence
of a society to unfold before the gaze of an outsider. Ethnology
runs into hopeless dead ends—and always will—especially
when it remains satisfied with impressionistic touches, rule-of-
thumb judgments, and classical psychology.

Like so many others, Lamartine inevitably saw only so
much of the Orient as the Orient was willing to show of itself,
that is, fragments, stereotypes, and no more than certain aspects of the Muslim character. And by the same token he saw
what his unconscious projected and exactly what he was looking for. "A nation of philosophers," "wisdom," "silence and
indolence," an omnipresent piety, visible and palpable—well,
it was all there, but then again it was not.

On the whole, Lamartine's vision was a generous one, and it
encompassed some vital and complex elements of the Muslim
soul. He saw that Islamic resignation, for example, has something sublime and tragic about it, and that in its first impetus
Islam was a heroic religion.[13] He understood very well that the
Qur'an has a universal and a specific dimension, and he recognized the authenticity of the Prophet's message.[14]

But Lamartine outdid himself in his speculation on the
future of Islam and the world. Moënis Taha-Hussein claims that
Lamartine's thought is tainted with sentimental rationalism,
confused and contradictory mysticism, and naivete. Perhaps,
but it also has perspicacity and a sharp focus. Lamartine was not
an orthodox Christian but an independent thinker with religious sympathies. He sympathized with Islam as well, but

again, he was not prepared to embrace it. He was conscious of the historical relativity of religions qua concrete forms, but he recognized the absolute religious structure of the human soul and the perennial problem of transcendence. He undoubtedly had faith in universal reason, but this was in no way a narrow, desiccated rationalism, since God looms on the horizon at every step in reason's progress. Lamartine grants that in matters of piety Christianity is to some extent superior to Islam, but he argues that from the standpoint of the history of religion Islam is more highly evolved than Christianity because it arrived at a later stage in the development of monotheism, and hence is more abstract, more streamlined, and more rational: "It is practical and contemplative theism. The sort of men who believe in it cannot be converted: one moves from a dogmatic system full of miracles toward a simpler kind of dogma, not the other way around." And, replying to Vigny who had characterized Islam as a "corrupt form of Christianity," Lamartine argues that it is rather "a purified form of Christianity." He still believes, however, that Muslim fatalism blights all of man's energies, and beyond that it is plain that Islam is in a state of utter decadence.

That is why Lamartine advocates the colonization (which will have, he imagines, a life-giving effect) of the Middle East, and sketches the scenario for what actually did take place, not in the Orient but in the Maghrib; that is, a direct colonization that had no effect at all on Islam as a religion, contenting itself with political domination and social interference. But Lamartine was talking about a grand sort of commerce between civilizations, not mere opportunistic politics. Nationalism, he said, tends to usurp the bonds of religion, but it is doomed to grow progressively weaker, because nothing can match the power of religion to fuse a society together. From that point of view the Middle East is badly fragmented, and hence faces immense difficulties in fashioning itself into one great nation. This analysis is double-edged, of course, and intuitively addresses a couple of major issues: the substitution of a national ideal for ideological and cultural ideals, and the necessary resurgence of the latter in a second stage.

Gérard de Nerval was intellectually akin to Lamartine, although in certain ways he had a more precise and comprehensive mind, while in others his development landed him in a mystical—and morbid—syncretism. Nerval's important *Travels in the Orient* (1851) can be broken down into three thematic clusters: themes dealing with the Muslim character, themes concerning morals, customs, and social practices and, finally, philosophical views on the essence of religion, relations between Christianity and Islam, and the future of Islam. The second cluster is perhaps the one that most commands our interest today. By and large Nerval reaffirms the old notions of Islamic vices and virtues, but his understanding of the whole situation shows some progress: aspects of character and forms of comportment are not treated in isolation but within a broad context that explains them without always managing to justify them.

Nerval's vision is colored by a comprehensive sympathy, a willingness to play the game and immerse himself in the human ambiance, an impeccable logic, at once serene and warm-hearted; and Moënis Taha-Hussein does justice to these qualities. But Nerval was not slow to spot some unpleasant facts: the greed of Turkish officials, the social conservatism, the fanatical exclusiveness of lower-class people in the cities (assuming all foreigners were Christians and prohibiting them from visiting the mosques), and the fatalism.

On the positive side, Nerval underlines such specific features as hospitality, nobility, pride (all Bedouin contributions to Oriental sensibility), equality, humility, humanity (the legacy of Islam), tolerance, and sensuality (whose purely institutional, almost juridical origins he never even suspected). Nerval presents these traits in an undifferentiated lump; and, like his predecessors, he fails to do the kind of detailed breakdown that would have made his analysis more useful. But, despite this defect and others, he does throw himself into the life of the Oriental peoples, apparently without surrendering for a moment his European identity or, still less, his attachment to French civilization. On the contrary, in the face of a world that day after day struck him as strange and even absurd, he felt just how deeply rooted he was in the West.

Nerval's philosophical and religious ideas have been the subject of a great deal of debate. Messiaen[15] confers on him an equivocal Christian status bordering on heresy, whereas Albert Béguin takes him to be an authentic Christian in search of himself.[16] In a series of articles, Louis Massignon argues that Nerval "wished to Islamicize his Christian heterodoxy by going to live in the Arabian Orient," adding "Gérard de Nerval's imagination came to Islam through an attraction that was more magnetic than magical."[17] For Massignon the problem of Nerval and Islam basically comes down to the problem of the influence of the Muslim imagination on the Western imagination. Lastly, Taha-Hussein's careful analysis has shown the heroic attempt Nerval made to build up for himself a fantastic religious syncretism, an effort at union with God that was destined to tragic failure.

This quest went far beyond the framework of *Travels in the Orient* and, paradoxically, it paid little heed to Islam. That may have been because Nerval exaggerated the positive, practical, realistic side of Islam, as opposed to the extreme idealism of Christianity, which he considered dangerous. I am convinced that Nerval, who was an archetypal Western deviant, was striking out for different human and spiritual shores from those of his own society, that he went on an existential voyage to Islam —to an Islam which, alas, could offer him nothing at that time.

Our rapid survey of French romanticism and Islam has now shifted from remote, even hostile thinking to vital commitment (however frustrated and unfruitful in Nerval's case). This constitutes real progress. Our analysis has included a number of strictures on the French romantic vision of Islam, and a few more need to be added. The most important is not that the Romantics were working with insufficient information. Quite the contrary, a newcomer on a scene, lacking both an insider's knowledge and bias, may make a better observer than someone whose mind is already made up. But that was not always the case with those writers who, although ignorant of the Orient's achievements and the scholarly works about them, were very much aware of Western images of the East. Hence one always senses a certain conventionality in the Romantic accounts. Those writers can also be faulted for neglecting the serious forces of renewal then secretly fermenting throughout the Arab world. Nerval merely loses himself in the crowd so as to bring back some picturesque reportage: he says not a word about the struggles by Muhammad Ali and Ibrahim Pasha to rebuild Egypt and foster Arab unity, nothing at all about the intellectual transformation and the open-mindedness toward modernity represented by the fumbling efforts of the *Nahda*. The same goes for Lamartine, although he had a stronger presentiment about the aspirations and torments of that still decadent but already awakened universe. We may note in passing that one of the leitmotives of Western contact with the Arab world will be the stress on things archaic and picturesque, the select attention paid to the forces of the past, as seen through the filter of popular experience. In the same way later generations of colonials, even though permanently installed in Islamic countries, would look at Islam as reflected in their lower-class attendants.

In their analyses the Romantic writers we have mentioned take for granted the existence, if not of a Muslim personality, at least of a Muslim character or, in vaguer terms, some observable psychic traits common to Muslims. But apart from the fact their period lacked an adequate conceptual and methodological apparatus (whence their rough-edged empiricism), their works present that "character" as all of a piece, lumping together components that are ancient but solidly in place and possibly ineradicable with historical accidents, not distinguishing present-day realities from the residue of the past. But then they never claimed to be historians of the *mentalités* school or social psychologists, only writers and artists.

### Profile of the Committed Intellectual

France can scarcely represent the entire West, but of all Western countries it is doubtless the one that had the most contact with Islam in the Mediterranean basin—and hence the one that opposed Islam most passionately. The Crusades were conducted mainly by French knights, and French colonization, unlike the English variety, involved pushing back the native population and "stocking" the colony with their own. This policy was harsh but, owing to the peculiar French love of universality, it was more intellectually stimulating than English methods. And just as there was always room in French political strategy for a working agreement with Islam, it seems that colonial and postcolonial France had at least a little room for love or understanding of Islam. We have seen an old tradition, limited to a minority but effective and persistent, beginning with Peter the Venerable and continuing on with Boulainvilliers, Napoleon—not the "Muhammad of the West," for he never had the Prophet's spirituality, but a sort of French Arab, a man of passion and moderation—and Lyautey, who was so fascinated by Islam's seigniorial values.

We have seen how nineteenth-century intellectuals like Lamartine and Nerval reached out to the Arab-Islamic world. After them, a certain number of literary works would draw upon Islam for their imagery (though they already had a colonialist tinge), but by this time Islam had been devalued, and now served as a natural setting for the weary consciousness of the West to refresh itself with a tough, artless wisdom. Yet the tradition of sympathy still survived. It was a refuge for the aristocratic mind, and we should not be surprised that figures like the Baron de Slane or the Comte de Gobineau—the first an admirer of Arabian culture, the second of Asiatic civilization—were aristocrats by birth and temperament, nor that Antoine de Saint-Exupéry and Louis Massignon were aristocratic in their instincts and attitudes. Generally speaking, these sympathetic tendencies arose out of admiration for the grandeur of classical Arabian civilization (with the underlying idea of challenging the widespread contemptuous prejudice toward the Arabs, since such disdain had now become a historical absurdity) and moved on to the discovery of a core of values incarnate in the Muslim as a human type.[18] Positive responses to Islam sometimes found

their *raison d'être* or their point of departure in a fervent personal
or mystical experience—with mystically minded individuals
looking to Islam in general and Persia in particular rather than to
the Arabs.

In any case this trend remained distinctly marginal to the
major currents of French thought and sensibility from the end of
the nineteenth century through the first third of the twentieth.
When people spoke of "the Orient," they now meant India and
China, whose arts captured the favor of the bourgeois, acquir-
ing a lofty status which Islam lost. French philosophy paid no
attention to Arab philosophy. Textbook treatments of monotheism were limited right from the start to the Judeo-Christian
tradition and, when a luminary like Henri Bergson took an
interest in Eastern mysticism, he focused his comprehensive
inquiry on Hinduism, never on Islam.[19] In effect Islam was too
close to Europe to stir up the enthusiasm that sends one's
thoughts off on an anxious journey toward truly foreign and
authentic shores. Islam, however, was too markedly autonomous in its affirmations to be annexed, subjugated, or taken
over piecemeal.

The fact is that French thought, which has contributed so
much to the making of history, has rarely proved capable of
understanding history, of sounding its vertiginous depths;
whereas German thought, which has shown itself singularly
inept at mapping out a reasonable, humane destiny for Germany, has studied, meditated on, grasped, and understood the
human adventure of history. Ever since the eighteenth century,
the French mind, with its abstract, juridical bent, has settled
into a universalizing rationalism. But a Voltaire or a Volney, for
all their prosaic realism, had a profound sense of the unity and
diversity of mankind. So did Lamartine, along with a love of
history that has, on the whole, been sadly deficient in French
literary thought. All three were genuine men of letters, and they
lived in an age when the intelligentsia felt "responsible."

The striking feature of French literature and philosophy in
the first third of the twentieth century was the absence of any
feeling for history. Measured against the eighteenth and

nineteenth centuries, it was a time of regression. French philosophers moved about in a sphere of empty generalities, while professional historians were trapped in their fields of specialization. But nowadays, and for the past thirty years, though the littérateurs and philosophers (the cutting edge of the French intelligentsia) may have shed little light on history's inner truths, they have done meritorious service as midwives to history in the making. They have injected morality into politics and shaped the thinking of the average person through the values that they disseminate. Though anonymous and confused, their influence has been real and historically important. Its core is the continued affirmation of certain irreducible human values. This capacity for affecting the consciousness (and conscience) of the public, this humanism playing its part on the stage of history, is the heart of French intellectual tradition.

It is altogether different from the great intellectual tradition of Germany, which displayed marvelous skill in reading the drama of the past, but either never acted on its own (slavishly conforming to the forces that ruled society in its day) or else exerted a mistimed and wrongheaded influence.[20] Rousseau's thought is less profound than Hegel's, but it provoked the French Revolution. The average French intellectual today is a strongly moral idealist and a political *naif*, but he or she is also a significant unconscious agent of progress. Thus, over the last twenty-five years the French intelligentsia has vigorously supported national liberation movements among the Arabs. In so doing they testified to the crucial fact that a given group of individuals can rise up, in the name of truth and morality, against the state, can crack the monolithic cohesiveness of the collectivity and break with the herd mentality. These progressive intellectuals are systematically antiracist. In their eyes the Arab has become the archetypal victim of persecution, the dog whom colonialists treat as a dog only because he is human, to borrow Sartre's felicitous expression.[21] This is not at all to say that French intellectuals have integrated the Arab past into their pattern of values or made Arab culture an organic part of the universality they profess. The "Arab" they defended was simply an abstract phenomenon, an item in their planetary messianic enterprise, an operation blending generosity, pride, and utopianism in equal proportions.

Yesterday the war in Algeria was their war, tomorrow the revolution in Latin America will have been their revolution. Hence we may wonder to what extent the French intelligentsia was willing and able to see anything in the Mahgrib liberation movements except a pure revolutionary action, cut off from its Arab-Islamic roots. This led to bitter disillusionment and, for some burningly militant souls, the shattering of intense hopes for brotherhood, a brotherhood without a fatherland, or rather with no other fatherland than that slice of contemporary life, that layer of history still reverberating with a common struggle and common dreams, free from the old historical categories.

But the task of building a state is quite obviously not the same thing as carrying out a revolution, and abstract universalism necessarily gives way in the face of resurgent populism and a reaffirmed corporate personality. To be sure, the fund of sympathy accumulated by the independence movements, the networks of friendship linking the Mahgrib states, on one side, with the French intellectual class and leftists on the other, are still intact, though badly shaken. But even sympathetic French observers—with some recent exceptions—blanch every time they hear proponents of Islam and Arab identity. Such people, for their part, realize that the principles of humanism, of human dignity and freedom (once the inspiration for support by French liberals) are openly flouted by rulers today not only in the Maghrib and other Arab countries, but practically everywhere in the Third World. The persecuted have become persecutors.

No doubt the French intellectual, so long as he remains one, and the Arab intellectual or revolutionary, so long as he holds the reins of power, can no longer share the same vision of the world—if in fact and in their heart of hearts they ever did. The man in power gradually learns to recognize and measure daily necessities, the breadth of the social spectrum, the compelling obligation to compromise and choose, and he become familiar with another kind of psychology. He turns into a "realist" and gets locked into a dialectic of the present or the near future. Sometimes his anxiety to be realistic sweeps him overboard and makes him lose sight of reality. Above all, his concern shifts from merely governing to maintaining himself in power, which changes his whole pattern of action. Meanwhile the French intellectual insists on being his old self—a conscientious champion of lofty values.

As far as external appearances go, Arab political leaders speak the language of a humanism derived from the West and in particular from France. This convention has by now spread far and wide: one also finds it in the communist world where the concepts of freedom, progress, and constitutional government are constantly affirmed to be the operative principles of political faith. But what sets the two groups so radically apart, what causes so much misunderstanding, what makes astonishment turn into malaise and then condemnation, is that Western intellectuals and even a good many politicians really believe in this universal humanism, whereas Arab and Third World rulers (and for a long time those from the communist world, despite their conversion to another kind of humanism) profess their belief in it without any inner conviction.

At this point I have left behind the main focus of my analysis in order to cast some light on the vague malaise afflicting the moral and intellectual conscience of France over the violent behavior of both the leaders and the masses in Arab countries and the Third World. The French are unwilling, and rightly so, to renounce their earlier efforts on behalf of colonial emancipation, a major achievement that made room for more actors on the stage of history. And besides, it is certain that the West exported to the outside world its technology of power and historical violence, its ideological and political structures. These were combined with abruptly rediscovered local traditions, and forced to adapt to a different personality type, giving them the look of Western institutions cut adrift in time. All this may explain why thoughtful Frenchmen refuse to see anything but

aberrations in what is, on the contrary, the deepest sort of
reality, carefully hidden from the scrutiny of that external
superego, the European observer.

The malaise nonetheless persists, though veiled by ambivalence. It bursts out into the open every time continuous and
direct contacts occur, when people discover the other in his
concrete particularity, beyond mere political categories. Then
we see a peculiar reserve, a psychic split, with inner suspicions
and outer protestations of solidarity. This is the same ambivalence that appeared at about the time of the 1967 Arab-Israel war
among progressive French intellectuals (one clear example
being Sartre) and various reflective individuals everywhere.
Arab threats, even verbal ones, against Israel's existence raised
the specter of a dangerous and hitherto unimaginable monolithic energy. It may be that unconscious associations between
the cult of force and the Arab soul took on a new vigor, old
images revived; they were always held in check, but only with
difficulty. Fears of Arab "frenzy" and "irrationality" awakened, and the idea that the Arabs were seriously disturbed
became lodged in the dim regions of the subconscious.

Nowadays, Western attitudes are more serene. And, in any
case, to the degree that Islam represents a religion of once
oppressed peoples, the politically committed intellectual will
have scruples about making a frontal attack on it, except in
concert with Muslims who are sick of Islam. All Western positions on Islam are connected to the dialectic of politics—the
Arabs and Israel, the Arabs and the West, Iran and its Marxist
opposition, Indonesia and its massacre of communists. No one
considers the past or future role of Islamic civilization in the
evolution of humanity. Only Islamicists and other "insiders,"
along with refugees from modernity ask themselves about the
values that Islam can contribute to our cloudy common future.
But elsewhere is the Muslim world taken seriously as such?
Does it have a message to convey? While American universities
open their doors to the best minds in Islam, the French university remains singularly resistant to any other approach but
paternalism. In the meantime Parisian intellectuals take

advantage of the de facto superiority their society enjoys and set themselves up as savant-dictators of the whole Mediterranean world.

In the nineteenth century a debate started between Jamal al-Din al-Afghani and Ernest Renan. Today French philosophers deliberately ignore the Arab intellectual renaissance now going on in their own language. Is this a jealously guarded monopoly of knowledge and intelligence, or cultural parochialism, or both? If the best minds in contemporary France were to extend a brotherly hand to Muslim intellectuals, it might lead to far broader and more probing discussions than those one hears up and down the boulevards of a provincial civilization.

# 3

# European Scholarship and Islam

The nineteenth century was the era of positivism, of critical historiography, of exegesis, and of Orientalism. And one brilliant thinker incarnated all these rationalistic aspirations in his own life: Ernest Renan. Renan was an Orientalist par excellence, but only as a Hebraist—or, speaking more generally, as a Semiticist—and an anti-Semitic one at that, to quote Massignon. He was hardly an expert on Islam, but he took a close interest in it, and his lecture on "Islam and Science" continues to be commented on, quoted, approved, and refuted.[1] His thesis, as a matter of fact, dealt with *Averroes and Averroism*.[2] Still readable today, it is a masterpiece of erudition, intelligence, and scholarly method. Finally, one can find reflections on Islam scattered here and there throughout his writings, from *The Future of Science* (one of his earliest works, though published very late)[3] through his obituary of Quatremère[4] to the *Memories of Childhood and Youth*.[5]

Renan's ideas about Islam did not evolve over the years; the most that can be said is that he clarified and systematized them in his famous lecture. Islam aroused his interest almost exclusively as a phase in the history of the human mind, which he considered the key to history in the broad sense. In itself "that degraded world" was unworthy of "the same painstaking study that we devote to the noble remains of the genius of Greece, ancient India, and Judea," but it formed part of man's tradition, whose pages, "even the saddest, call for interpreters."[6] Theocratic societies (of which Islam was the most widespread model, although the Papal States, which also came in for some denunciation, confined its wrongdoing to a small space) were a blight on the flowering of intelligence, a crushing counterattack on reason, and hence a historical evil.

Renan did not assault Islam in itself, in its specific religious and moral identity. Nor did he slip into the old Christian habit of belittling the Muslim adversary. One good thing about positivistic rationalism is that it puts all religions on the same level by refusing to adhere to any of them. And beyond this, Renan's own approach was neither narrow nor opposed, in principle, to all religious ideas per se. In his *Memories* he admits how much he owed, in human and moral terms, to Saint-Sulpice—in both what he enjoyed and what he renounced he remained a Christian. By the same token, he acknowledges that Islam always stirred up deep emotions in him, to the point that he never entered a mosque without regretting that he was not a Muslim. Thus the severe grandeur of Islam as a religion awakened feelings in him altogether different from the repulsion that the Orient as such caused "by its pomp, its ostentation, its impostures."

Renan the historian and philosopher was aware of religion's contribution to humanity's effort to overcome its infirmities. Which is to say that although his vision of Islam's role in history is perhaps incompetent and most certainly unjust and too sketchy, it distorts reality less than his detractors would claim. At any event, Renan does not expel Islam from the great religious tradition of humanity.

He does, however, hold it squarely responsible for enchaining the Oriental mind and for blocking the development of science in Middle Eastern countries. Renan looks at the problem of Islam primarily as an intellectual historian. The title of his lecture, "Islam and Science," eloquently suggests the orientation of his critical analysis.

The Arab race, he argues, was at first the leading force in Islamic society. Preoccupied with the conquest and organization of an empire, it was strongly "antipathetic to Greek philosophy" and to rational activity. "Trapped like all the Semitic peoples within the tight circle of prophecy and poetic enthusiasm," it was interested in neither science nor philosophy.[7] There was no extraordinary development in either field until the day when the Abbasid dynasty opened up to Persia, which belonged to the Indo-European race and knew how to keep its genius alive. From the ninth to the eleventh century in the Orient and from the eleventh to the end of the twelfth century in Spain, Muslim civilization filled a terrible void and illuminated the human mind, reworking and enriching the heritage of Greece to pass it on to Europe. But this philosophical legacy, as Renan saw it, had nothing to do with the Arabs or Islam.

It came into its own, as a matter of fact, just when Arab predominance in Islamic civilization was drawing to a close. The Arabs had ignored everything but poetry and linguistics, the two cardinal and, one might say, exclusive poles of their peculiar genius. If Arabic was used as a vehicle for philosophy, that was because it managed to assert and maintain itself as the language of high culture, exactly as Latin did in the Middle Ages. Like Roger Bacon, who wrote in Latin but was not Latin himself, Avicenna wrote in Arabic without being an Arab. The Arabian peninsula was no more responsible for so-called Arabian philosophy than Latium was for medieval scholasticism.

Arabian philosophy, it turns out, is not even Islamic. It saw the light of day only because of the Syrians, the Harranians, and the Nestorians, the fossilized remnants of the ancient Hellenic world and the custodians of its treasures. The Abbasid dynasty encouraged them in their monumental labors of translation and adaptation because it was not burdened by the weight of crude Arabian folkways, because the civilizing syncretism that animated its first rulers guided their concerns toward regions untouched by the central inspiration of Arabism.

But the key factor here was that the oppressiveness of Islamic religion and theology had not yet impinged upon the structure of the state. Religion had not yet succeeded in laying its heavy chains on either the public authorities and their entourage or on the masses, which would later be so thoroughly Islamized. At that time the moving force in scientific endeavors came from a non-Islamic enclave (Harranians and Nestorians), and the political agents who protected it were undisturbed by pressure from Islam. Finally, at the height of its classical period, "Muslim" philosophy was represented by de-Islamized thinkers: though Avicenna never lacked a certain amount of fideism, this was largely counterbalanced by his rationalism, as well as by the whole cast of his personal and moral life, freed from religious taboos.[8] There can be no doubting that Averroes was a materialist. If he did not, as the story has it, cry out in parody of Balaam, "Let me die the death of the philosophers," his thought at least fashioned a basically nonreligious world, without, however, explicitly denying Revelation. Renan describes *falsafa* as evolving outside the Islamic sphere, as cultivated by a small minority and subject to persecution from the twelfth century on—in short, as something that Islamic culture, despite its comprehensive breadth, regarded as a foreign body.

Actually, the most representative products of the Islamic spirit, for all the bitter factional splits they have caused, are the sectarian speculations so fully portrayed in the many treatises on heresy. Kharijism, Shiism and its branches, *kalam* and *Asharism*—these are the dynamic principles of authentic Islam. Born out of internal need, containing all kinds of symbioses of religion and culture, unfolding through endogenous efforts, sects and heresies remain a direct outgrowth of Revelation, part of the central tradition of Islam. Such is not the case with *falsafa*.

With its non-Islamic content it was only tolerated in the first centuries of the Hijra (ninth to twelfth century A.D.) because Islam lacked the strength to control or, rather, to stifle it. But in the second phase of its development (from the thirteenth century on) the reactionary forces of fanaticism underlying Islam penetrated the whole fabric of society and won a decisive victory over freedom of thought. An inquisition of sorts imposed its violent norms, claiming Averroes as its most illustrious victim.

Then there was the geopolitical factor: the invasion of un-civilized, barbarian peoples (Berbers and Turks in particular), who held the reins of power in Islamic society. "At the outset Islam, weakened by the sects and tempered by a kind of Prot-estantism (known as Motazelism) was much less organized and fanatical than in its second period, when it fell into the hands of the Tartars and Berbers, two races that were gross, brutal, and mindless."[9]

Islamic philosophy, therefore, existed not because but in spite of Islam, just as Western science developed in the face of resistance from the Catholic church. Hence there can never be a scientific and philosophical renaissance among Muslim nations until the pressure exerted by religion is neutralized. That is the way he recommends for any future regeneration, in his answer to Jamal al-Din al-Afghani, a document fairly bristling with the naive racism of his day: "The Muslims," he declares, "are the first victims of Islam." Just as Europe had done (except for Spain, which was still living in the Middle Ages), they must now break the chains of religious tyranny.[10]

Renan's vision is at once simplistic and complex.[11] The idea that Islamic culture has passed through two stages, with the second ending in stagnation, has been widely accepted for some time. But was this the decline of an entire civilization or simply a cultural setback? In either case, Renan's explanation remains superficial, because we cannot be sure that the stranglehold of orthodoxy on political, intellectual, and social life brought on the long depression of Islamic culture. It would make more sense to speak of many convergent factors leading to the con-traction of Islamic civilization—a contraction that undoubtedly worked to safeguard it and guarantee its permanence.

As far as freedom of thought goes, the admirable creative outpouring of the tenth and eleventh centuries testifies to the unfathomable riches of Islamic culture. The fact that revolu-tionary currents such as Kharijism and Qarmatism existed at all,

that they assaulted politico-religious orthodoxy, that some
philosophers were able to transcend the mentality (Islamic,
Christian, or otherwise) of their age, that a man like Abu-al-Ala
al-Maari, in his lonely isolation, could proclaim his unbelief
(and countless others thought as he did)—all this dramatically
belies the usual notions about the monolithic character of Islam
as well as the idea that the richness of Islam derives from Muhammad by a kind of strict deductive logic. Renan too was
partly taken in by these fallacies because he failed to define
correctly either Islam or *arabisme* (what we might call Arab identity). He equated Islam with its theological apparatus and specifically with the triumphant orthodoxy of the twelfth century.
He reduces Arab identity to the narrow confines of the Bedouin
population of the Arabian peninsula, as it burst upon the world
in the seventh century.

This vision of history is quite static. "Arabness" is not an
ethnic concept, even if it originally was one. It is the cultural
melting pot where the most varied forms of human genius
joined together, the interpretive medium through which they
expressed themselves. As for Islam, it remains, it is true, first
and foremost a religion (however diversely understood). But in
its unconscious depths as well as in its loftiest manifestations it
strongly influenced the lives of men and women. Avicenna and
Averroes were thus the products not only of Islamic civilization
but purely and simply of Islam, both by their education and in
their fidelity to a historical human community. And it is false to
say that the foundations of *falsafa* were laid by non-Muslims.

With regard to the obscurantist role played by religion, that
is too broad a theme to be dealt with systematically here. In
Europe, certainly, scientific and philosophical rationalism met
with spirited opposition from the Church in the sixteenth and
seventeenth centuries, and staked out its independence from
the teachings of religion and existing university institutions. In
eighteenth-century France a radical critique of religion—closely
tied in its ideals and habits to the ancient world—ushered in the
modern mentality. In Germany this was accomplished by a

philosophy that had at least partly shaken off the grip of religion. But such a revolt was in each case bound up with profound
transformations in society, politics, and ways of thinking. The
birth of the modern world required four whole centuries of
struggle and toil in the West. It was a global enterprise, one of
those crucial periods in human history when the destiny of man
was totally redefined. It cannot be described merely as a return
to antiquity or the closing of a supremely religious medieval
parenthesis.

For the first time since civilization began, people broke free
from religion and from the weight of the unseen, just as they
were gaining mastery over nature, and the individual was
emerging on the scene. Not only did Islamic culture contribute
to all this through a whole series of scientific advances (which
Renan really never mentions) but it safeguarded the Greek heritage, and from the ninth to the sixteenth century it defended the
preeminence of that heritage. If it is true that humanism and the
spirit of the Renaissance in the West were launched only by
returning to Greece by way of the Arabs, then the latter had the
virtue, from the Western standpoint at least, of preserving, all
through the age of scholasticism, the abstract idea and concrete
tradition of an ancient, non-Christian culture as a source of
rational knowledge. Generally speaking, Islam mixes religion
with culture. It sees religion as linked to the power of what has
been written and thought, as creating by its very existence a sort
of productive turmoil in the mind. That is why dialectical ap-
proaches to reality have often considered Islam, like the
Church, a barrier holding back the barbarians.

European liberal humanism could never have been simply
deduced from classical antiquity, as if it were premised on ancient thought, without the double mediation, positive and negative, of Christianity.[12] Positive, because the message of the
Gospels has left a permanent mark on Western man and has
been stored up in the collective unconscious; negative, because
the oppressive hand of the Church has dialectically provoked its
antithesis. The same holds for European rationalism, which at

once denied and gave fresh impetus to religion. It is striking, by the way, how often the great rationalists are rooted in a clerical milieu. Historical erudition is deeply indebted to the Bollandists, and the Jesuits (who counted Voltaire and Diderot among their pupils) propagated the classical culture rediscovered by the Renaissance. Kant bore the traces of his mother's pietism, Hegel was at first a philosopher of religion, and Renan himself was a former seminarian.

In a certain sense I agree with Renan in thinking that no cultural and scientific renewal can grow out of the Greco-Roman heritage so long as one lets the categories and particular methods of that heritage direct the quest for understanding. Nevertheless a renaissance is unthinkable without a solid ancient base, the object of study, pride, and reclamation efforts. Generally speaking, I too advocate the liberation of Islamic society and the individuals in it from the influence of religion. But present-day conditions are no carbon copy of the European situation from the sixteenth to the eighteenth century, along with the speedup of the process in the nineteenth century. My whole thesis explicitly states that a new approach has to be made to the problem of Arab-Muslim destiny, namely a dialectical interplay between the archaic and the modern. In this vein I have postulated a new Islam entity by integrating the ideological and cultural personalities that synthesize and bring up to date both the deposits of the archaic past and the forward thrust into modernity. To be purely modern is to be forever tearing down and building up with no solid base to work on, and every collective destiny requires some inertia.[13]

The failure of Atatürk serves as proof that history made somewhere else cannot be artificially repeated, that at all costs one must not cut off a social body from its energy sources. Here we see the fundamental problem of causing a break in the historical continuum. France is the classic European example of a break with the past followed by an attempt to retrieve it. But in the case of Islam this pattern might not necessarily have to precede any effort at synthesis, and it might not have to be pressed to the bitter end—to hostility and destruction.

I have argued in another context that Islam has shown a tendency to choke off internal conflicts, presenting a unified front to the world, sometimes by using violence.[14] In the social sphere, for example, the feudal system was not set up in Western fashion, a true bourgeoisie failed to materialize and, although Islamic guilds did foster the ideology of a militant opposition, we find nothing like the struggles that exploded in the communes of fourteenth-century Flanders.

In religious matters, the representatives of Islamic orthodoxy never matched the Inquisition in organized oppression, just as the *fuqaha* class, however closely associated with the powers that were during the second period of Islam, did not invest itself with the authority of the Church. Islamic history has never stood still, but beneath the external restlessness of changing monarchies and a confused political life, it displayed a great deal of stability, thanks to the way it neutralized opposing forces and disarmed deep-seated antagonisms.

Paradoxically, Islam as a religion lacks Christianity's power of systematic self-defense. Experience shows that every time the state or other social and cultural forces fascinated by the myth of modernity raise their hand against it, Islam threatens to collapse. The internal dynamism that attracted followers to Islam from all over the world operates in such a way that it survives, and fights for its survival alone, without any organizational underpinnings, any specific social class protecting it, or any formal apologetics.

Owing to both a singular historical dialectic and to that fundamental dynamism, Renan's insistent prophecy that the regeneration of Islamic countries depended upon the rejection of Islam has not come true, at least not as he envisioned it.

## The Psychology of Orientalism

### A Double Marginality

Though an Orientalist, Renan's writings, his influence, and the whole tenor of his life give him a place at the center of the nineteenth-century European intellectual tradition. His harsh treatment of Islam is tied in with a grand egalitarian vision of cultural progress. In the final analysis the religious state and religious oppression are stages of human development through which Europe itself has passed, at considerable cost, and from which it has won deliverance.

This was not the approach of Orientalists who were experts on Islam. They affirmed their European identity as a kind of solid front to counter a monolithic, unchanging Islam. Indiscriminately invoking now Christianity, now contemporary secularism, they accused Islam either of spiritual deficiency or of theocratic rigidity. The classical Orientalist is thus the most radical of Westernizers, as if contact with a foreign culture sharpened his sense of being different and so, anxious at the prospect of losing this difference (or of sinking in the undertow of another, inferior world), he made a point of asserting it more vigorously. Contact between cultures always makes for drama: an ontological, communal drama of human differences or an existential, intellectual drama in the life of an individual. Superficial contact creates a feeling of strangeness; more profound encounters risk bringing on the dissolution of the self, the shattering of its coherence, the end of certitude, and a traumatic challenge to one's values.

Seeking perhaps to head off these dangers, the Orientalist ensconces himself in the superiority of things European. Whereas the critically minded intellectual harbors doubts about his own society, and the ethnologist sometimes tries to flee it, the Orientalist assigns an exemplary status to the destiny of Europe. And in so doing he locks Islam into an exclusive confrontation with the West. The history of Islam no longer unfolds according to its own inner dynamic but is seen as a pale, reversed image of Western history. To take a crucial example, analyses of Muhammad's personality all reveal an implicit comparison with Christ. If Muhammad was insincere—or if the question of his sincerity is raised to begin with—it is because Christ was sincere. If he was sensual and a polygamist, it is because Jesus was chaste. If he was a warrior and politician, this judgment implies a peace-loving Jesus, defeated and crucified.

The paradox of the Orientalist studying Islam is that while standing apart from the mainstream of the Western intellectual tradition, he nonetheless sets himself up as a spokesman for the West. That is why on one hand, thoughtful Arabs who have been genuinely Westernized, whether in their ideological vision of the world or in their methodological training, can at least oppose such Orientalism as an inauthentic product of the West and at most regard it as a phase in a worldwide historical process, when relations between East and West were governed by the ideology of colonialism. On the other hand, "pure" Arab thinkers, who are not looking for any spiritual or intellectual authority outside their own culture, reject the approach taken by Orientalists as malevolent, superficial, and alien.

Such is the ambiguity of his situation that the Orientalist does not know, all things considered, what public he is speaking to. For the most part the West pays no attention to Islam, except in a marginal way, so that in addressing a Western audience the Orientalist simplifies, popularizes, and cheapens the substance of what he knows. The tenuous rigging that supports an entire universe collapses or goes awry. Its central character and essential purpose are obscured. And the naive affirmation of the collective Western personality only makes things worse.

In contrast, when he speaks in a strictly Islamic context, the Orientalist puts himself at the heart of his subject. What was peripheral becomes central, subsidiary elements are transformed into key factors. Because humanity has no one, single homeland, the study—and above all the historical study—of particular societies and cultures can never be a disembodied and nonlocalized science. But for this very reason the Orientalist, acting in the name of science, lays a brutal hand, sometimes even a malicious one (in the case of Lammens, for example) on something that is not simply an inert object of knowledge but a living reality that people have loved, committed themselves to, loaded down with their suffering and their fidelity—the foundation, in the most intimate sense, of their selfhood. In a Middle Eastern context, then, the Orientalist finds another kind of marginality: what is irrelevant now is not his subject, but his approach.

Had it not been for this reciprocal mistrust, Orientalism might have helped enormously to demythologize the heroic vision of Islam in the same way that liberal exegesis has demythologized the biblical era or the history of Christianity. Science has an extraordinary erosive power that we must accept if we are not to cut ourselves off from the dialectic of history. But that dialectic acknowledges the existence of a shadowy zone beyond the reach of abstract science that will not passively endure invasion. Progress, therefore, can no longer be gauged by the degree to which one abandons or denies oneself. In other words, the need to maintain one's identity has to be balanced or conjoined with the rights of truth, assuming for the moment that Orientalism has always dwelt in the realm of timeless, serene, objective truth.

## *From Islamophobia to Arabophobia*

The Europe which Orientalism has in mind is a medieval Christian Europe, as if that world had not been swept away by the whirlwind of revolution in the nineteenth century. And Europe's notion of the psychology of Islam is similarly static. It conjures up before our eyes simple, fixed human types: the Arab, the Muslim, the Berber, the Turk, all endowed with stable, rather too stable, characters. Likewise, all the richness of Islamic "culture" disappears into a descriptive picture based not on patient analysis but on intuitions aiming to reveal the essence of that culture at a glance. Certain incapacities, congenital blindspots so to speak, become apparent. An incapacity, for instance, " 'to see life steadily and see it whole,' to understand that a theory of life has to match all the facts, and a tendency to be stamped with a single idea while being blind to everything else . . ." as MacDonald says.[15] An incapacity to grasp the non-utilitarian nature of knowledge, as MacDonald and Von Grune-

baum argue.[16] An incapacity for science, for technology, or for
rationality, a theme developed by Abel and Bousquet.[17] The list
of Islam's weaknesses goes on and on.

By placing this sharp emphasis on the overwhelming phenomenon of Europe, the most biased sort of Orientalism forfeits
any claim to universality and flees the risky dynamics of real
contact. But even serious Orientalism—basically aligned with
the German tradition—has failed to discover the critical linkage
point between the inner essence and the outer appearance of a
culture. In studying the history of Islam, it ascribes too large a
role to minorities, Christian, Jewish, or otherwise. The social
historian turns his attention to the status of these minorities
much as the cultural historian looks to encounters with foreigners, to outside influences, to areas of intermingling—precisely
where whatever is thoroughly Oriental, Arab, or Islamic fades
away. Becker goes so far as to reduce Islamic civilization to a
progressively Asiaticized form of Hellenism.

But whereas Becker offers a panoramic view of human history and its underlying inner connections, Lammens debases
his subject by trying to banish Islam altogether. Lammens's
work is marked by endless regret for the Arab victory in the
seventh century, which inaugurated an era of contraction or
dissolution for eastern Christianity. On the one hand, he sym-
pathizes spontaneously with all the powers that opposed Islam
(or that he thinks opposed it); for example, the Umayyad dynasty. On the other hand, he pours out his venom on the family of
the Prophet, especially on ʿAli, whom he presents as the incar-
nation of the new Islamic ideal, the baneful factor whom the
resurgence of ancient forces, quite fortunately, stopped cold, at
least for a time. Lammens maintains that the Umayyads reestab-
lished ties with the Bedouin traditions which were most alien to
the new religion, that they reaffirmed a social continuity, giving
pride of place to the anti-Islamic Quraysh aristocracy, in a word,
that they exercised their power in an arena that was objectively
neutral but subjectively hostile to the religious core of Islam.
Because of all this, Lammens treats the Umayyads as noble
heroes who resisted the evil curse of revolution and imposture.

The same kind of distortion can be found in Dozy, whose analysis of the Harra incident fairly bristles with hatred. In 682 the citizens of Medina rebelled against Caliph Yazid I in the name of Islam. In order to subdue them the Caliph dispatched one of his most brutal generals, Muslim b. ʿUqba al-Murri, who put down the rebellion. Among those killed were many sons of Muhammad's first companions but, despite that, the oldest Arab historians, such as Tabari and Baladhuri, report the affair rather calmly. Then in the middle of the nineteenth century Reinhart Dozy, a Dutch historian writing in French, gets all worked up, protests and fulminates, not out of compassion for the slain but in passionate support of Yazid's action.[18] In Dozy's view, Yazid crushed the arrogant, ideological Islam of the Prophet's city. The suppression of Harra is "the pagan principle reacting against the Muslim principle."[19] "The Arabs of Syria," he says, "settled their account with the sons of those sectarian fanatics who had flooded Arabia with the blood of their fathers." The ancient Meccan "nobility" had struck a lethal blow against the new Islamic "nobility" created by militant superiority in the realms of faith and conquest. Dozy cannot come up with language abusive enough for this new "class" and its members, for men like Husayn and ibn al-Zubayr.

Wellhausen long ago did justice to the truth in this matter, explaining that, as a historian who knew the texts, views like Dozy's were based on a totally false notion of the political history of early Islam.[20] Actually what we have here is something quite different from a bad reading of the documents. At bottom, Dozy's assumptions tie in with a fundamental pattern of the Western unconscious: in order to overcome the disturbing elements of the Orient's otherness, its crypto-Western features must be warmly encouraged—the Umayyad dynasty, Hellenism, certain features of Sufism (Hallajism is a "religion of the cross," etc.). Lammens and Dozy condemn the youthful power of nascent Islam in the name of the aristocratic spirit of pre-Islamic Arabia. Nowadays some Orientalists take the opposite approach, implicitly condemning contemporary Arab movements in the name of ancient Islam.[21] This school of thought is

carried by its love of Islam into hatred of Arabs. Islam is perceived to be a force promoting spirituality and humane balance,
whereas the Arab renaissance inherits the old indestructible,
frenetic messianism of the East.

The Islamophobic Orientalism of the late nineteenth and
the first half of the twentieth century and the Islamophilic
Orientalism of the second half of this century correspond to two
marginal moments of Western consciousness, which relate in
turn to two moments of Western history as a whole. In the first
instance there was a radiant, quasi-absolute faith in Western
values (a composite of humanism, Christianity, and rationality); in the second, there was doubt and even reprobation
vis-à-vis what might be considered the degeneracy and, at
worst, the radical despiritualization of the West.[22] The classic
Orientalist and the contemporary Orientalist thus differ widely
in their degree of commitment to their own time, but they unite
harmoniously in their internal affirmation of the same basic
values, crushed on one front and triumphant on another. And
Western humanism, the Christian variety in particular, finding
itself in distress and opening itself up to all forms of transcendence because of that distress, reaches out to Islam, as to a
long-hidden treasure now suddenly discovered, fearful that it
may go under in the current universal rout of the spirit.

So present-day Orientalism covers a gamut of positions,
and the one most hostile to Islam is only a single minority view.
Furthermore, during its evolution, Orientalism has not simply
kept an eye on developments in the West but has also adapted to
the immense fact of the political renaissance now sweeping the
Arab world. The very meaning of the work done by Orientalists
has unquestionably changed. This activity has given up its global ambitions and retreated to a purely intellectual sphere. In the
process, Orientalism has gained in scholarly precision what it
has lost in political and philosophical prestige. From now on the
"scientific study of the Orient" will progressively break down
into its various component disciplines. As the Arabs and Muslims in general become adept at modern methods of research, it

will cease to have any special *raison d'être*, except as a minor link in the chain of universal knowledge.

Because both the origins of Orientalism and at least one hundred years of its history (1850–1950) were conditioned by the Muslim world's incapacity for self-awareness, the very existence of Orientalism symbolized the era of inferiority and intellectual guardianship that the East was passing through.

Granting all that, Orientalism remains a grand venture on the part of the Western mind. Oppressive and imperialistic though it was, European civilization still had the curiosity to scan the length and breadth of the human race, and the merit of calling into question its own imperialism. And so the Orientalist point of view can be discredited without even leaving the framework of Western thought: on the level of methodology, its standards can be contrasted with the much greater rigor prevailing in the social sciences, and on the level of its overall thrust, which can be measured against the notions of the inherent logic of all cultures, of their value as alternate worlds, and their claim on the student's sympathy. The undeniable conservatism of Orientalist politics can be riddled by the ideological arsenal of liberalism, and so forth. But for all that it was and is a crucial first stage in the diffusion of, and the acclimatization to, the methods of modern scholarship throughout the Middle East.

## Themes of Orientalism

At this juncture we may take a quick look at some general ideas put forth by the serious kind of Orientalism, ideas that translate into a genuine vision of Islam. Western Orientalism has had a number of great thinkers, men unjustly ignored by their own society: Goldziher, for example, Becker, Wellhausen, and one of the greatest historians that the modern West has produced, a prophet as well as scholar, Massignon.

For Goldziher, the meaning of Muhammad's prophetic work lies in its overthrow of the ideals of *Jahiliyya*. Islam turns away from tribal humanism, *Muruwwa*, replacing it with a much broader religious ideal, *din*.[23] But Islam has also secularized religion by trying to found a kingdom of this world with the means of this world.[24] Politics thus entered religion and left its mark on it. At the outset Islam was a moral revolution; then in the Medina phase it turned into a warrior's religion. But this combativeness is not just the result of the historical vicissitudes surrounding the victory of Islam, which also reflect the influence of the distinctly aggressive Arab mentality. Hence the aggressive character of Islamic religion—its yearning to conquer, its exclusiveness, and certitude of possessing the truth—all constitute a continuation of the Arab spirit. Nonetheless Goldziher argues elsewhere that the essence of Islam is surrender to the will of God, submission, and dependency.

We find practically the same ideas in the writing of Snouck-Hurgronje. He too maintains that Islam "came into the world as a political religion, and owes its universal significance to this union of two theoretically incompatible factors."[25] He presents the Prophet as a sensitive man with a nervous temperament, a deviant from the prevailing morality of his native city and his times, a person aware of his superiority.

The theme of Islam's rejection of older ideals, along with psychological analysis of the Prophet's personality and the characterization of Islam as a combative religion, nourished the thinking of all Orientalists in the first half of the twentieth century. This approach was, in a way, a prolongation of the medieval vision of Islam, because it put the issues within a religious framework and assigned an eminent place to the Prophet. It is likewise an obvious instance of the inversion of Islamic history already pointed out: in particular, the depiction of Islam as a combative religion relates to the ideal Christian scheme of things. In his preaching, Christ has no use for politics, and his eternal glory is based on his earthly failure. The Church did not found an empire, it converted the already existing Roman Empire, and wormed its way into it. Postexilic Judaic tradition undoubtedly looked to the religious notion of the

Messiah as a compensation for worldly disaster, and, in line with this, the Church abandoned the Mosaic synthesis between the historical experience of Israel and its longing for God. But the prophets still tried to convert those in power, as we see from the career of John the Baptist. In another cultural sphere, namely Persia, Mazdak directed his preaching at the Sasanid monarchy. His efforts flourished for a time, thanks to the support of King Kavadh, but later came to nought when the king deserted him.

Painting cultural history with a rather broad brush, Becker treats Islam as an offshoot of Hellenism, the same Hellenism that, he says, produced Christianity. Becker returns to the old idea advanced by John Damascene in the eighth century that Islam is a heretical Christian sect, something like Arianism.[26] But among Western scholars Becker is outstanding for his insistence on the strictly religious nature of Islam, which he regards as aiming at salvation in the Beyond—an orientation that it borrowed from Christian Hellenism. What the latter could not successfully develop, however, Islam raised to a state of perfection, because "Islamic theocracy is the concrete manifestation of an ideal that Christianity had hitherto tried in vain to achieve."[27]

Until the European Renaissance of the sixteenth century, it was Islam that, in a manner of speaking, took over both the spiritual and cultural legacy of Hellenism (which it expressed in its own autonomous forms), while Europe lost touch with Hellenism, and proved incapable of assimilating and preserving its substance. Then there was a historical shift, or turnabout: Renaissance Europe rediscovered Hellenism and integrated into its world view a new conception of man and the self. The self-affirming individual is a purely Western creation. Meanwhile the other branch of Hellenism, Islam, not only did not come up with the same results, it ignored them: it ignored humanism as a support for civilizing values and it ignored the self. It has thus persisted as "an increasingly Asiatic form" of Hellenism. Islam remains essentially "a thorough mix of Greek intellectualism and Oriental contemplation." Hence salvation lies in a comprehensive Europeanization of Islamic culture. Since Islam has shown itself to be a severe hindrance to the blossoming of humanism, the best hope for its adherents would be to repudiate its powerful religious ties.

Any significant idea ought to prompt its audience to reflection and even make it uneasy. Becker's does both, although it clearly bears the impress of its time. He does not think that Islam can renew itself by turning to humanism. In his view Islamic society and culture ought to seek out a principle of regeneration alongside, or even outside, Islam, through massive imports of European humanism.

There is no denying that Hellenism has always been part of Islam, but Becker exaggerates the force of this presence. If one takes a global (and highly reductive) view of the situation, one may admit that Islam is only a new expression of Hellenism and of its other offshoot, Christianity. But the more closely one examines the facts—a product is not necessarily a copy, or else there would be no history—one realizes that Islam is a complex and original edifice.

It is true that the territory Islam invaded so tumultuously had been stamped by Hellenism—and this holds for regions once controlled by the Romans, Byzantines, and Sasanids. But it is equally true that in the first two cases we are talking about an enervated Hellenism, well on its way to extinction; and in the third, of a marginal, superficial Hellenism, since the Sasanid world had for some centuries before its collapse established its civilization on the base of an ancient Oriental heritage. The Orient had no choice but to find a *modus vivendi* with Islam (whereas Hellenism sought asylum in Byzantium and the West), and hence it became Islamicized at the same time that it Orientalized Islam.

From the first century of the Hijra onward the predominant tonality in the body and soul of Islam (that is, in its way of life, its culture and politics) was Oriental and not Hellenic. Only in the structure of its religious sensibility and intellectual insights did Islam carry on and enrich the Hellenic tradition. Its behavioral patterns of fear and compassion, its ascetical ideal, and its liturgical music were drawn from the rich resources of Mesopotamian Christianity; and, from the second to the sixth century of the Hijra, nonliterary Arab-Islamic intellectual activity can be traced directly back to Hellenism. But this Hellenism never fused with the central core of the culture and—this is crucial—the personality of Islam. For at the profound level where a culture recognizes what is its own and what is foreign to it, "classic" Arab-Islamic consciousness never recognized Hellenism as an integral part of its legacy and never saw it as destined to become such.

In the West, Hellenism was acknowledged before it was truly known. Eventually it was both known and acknowledged, only to be bypassed by a new tradition which had its own source of authority. This, in my opinion, is how Becker's thesis has to be corrected and explained. If I am right, Hellenism could evidently never have had any future in a society that refused to accept it as a basic ingredient of its personality and heritage. In contrast, though it was temporarily forgotten or driven underground in the West by the Barbarian invasions, as soon as circumstances permitted, Hellenism was free to make a resurgence. It could spring up again and flourish because it was one of the elements of the Western personality. Hence no medieval Christian censorship could ever have banished Aristotle, for example, from the realm of learning, however rigorously the logic of totalitarian religion might be applied. At most, the Church might distort him and then claim him for her own, but obviously it would not take long for him to break free, as he did.

In summary, the kind of Hellenism that we find in Islam during its primitive and classic periods (from the seventh to the eleventh century A.D.) can be considered a pseudo-Hellenism. And in any civilization a pseudo-principle, however fecund it may be, can only come to grief. Its glittering light will be snuffed out by the slightest setback. As a matter of fact, postclassical and modern Islam history (twelfth to nineteenth century) reveals a more and more assertive Orientalization as the most profound sort of cultural forces come into existence, whether on their own or by synthesizing with higher levels. One could almost claim that Islam and the Orient are identical, always excepting the Far East as constituted by Chinese tradition.

A final word on the subject of Orientalism. It differs from history, to be sure, in that history endeavors simply to understand any given society, not to put it on trial, while Orientalism arrogates the right to judge and ultimately to condemn and reject. But this feature may derive from its extremely vulnerable and uncomfortable position in a zone of otherness where the essence of a culture undergoes a deformation, where some bias or other has to emerge, where knowledge comes unstuck from both responsibility and real life. Orientalism is also, no doubt, a phenomenon provoked by the situation of Islam between 1860 and 1960: Islam was experiencing a crisis and lacked the intellectual and scholarly resources to analyze itself, though it had more than enough enthusiasm. So Orientalism filled the gap.

During that time, however, Islam was dominated by the West and, when the backlash came, Orientalism suffered. Not that it was, in general, the conscious agent of that domination. But its worst representatives gave aid and comfort to prejudice and at times even mirrored the coarsest sort of Western thinking. Thus it showed its inability to transcend its social and historical origins.

ETHNOLOGY

What can the ethnologist make of Islam? It would seem that the civilization called Islamic is too complex, too immersed in the flow of history, and too rich in its canon of classics to be a valid subject of ethnology, which works with simple structures and "primitive" societies. The most prominent areas, whether traditional or modern, of Islamic society are clearly the province of the sociologist and the historian. But on the fringes of that same society lie zones where man continues to struggle with nature and to live together with his fellows according to archaic norms, relying on the techniques of magic and functioning within a network of immemorial, irrational customs. Such was the case until recently with certain Bedouin tribes in Arabia, certain Berber groups in the Maghrib, with the Moors and Touaregs on the edge of the Sahara. And in fact, since the end of the nineteenth century, a more or less sound body of ethnological material has been built up concerning these marginal elements.[28] Their simple and autonomous culture could not be connected to traditional Arab-Islamic culture, and so was excluded from the epistemological scope of Orientalism.

But the ethnologist can survey any and all societies, including those in the West. Any given people may arouse astonishment and sympathy. All over the world we find pockets of uniqueness, archaic structures finding expression in customs, folklore, and ways of life.

Without realizing it, the early Arab travel-writers and geographers did ethnological work, both on Islamic culture and, more particularly, when they tried to explain non-Islamic manners and customs. Ibn Hawqal has some altogether remarkable passages on the Berbers and African Negroes. Muqaddasi, Idrisi, Ibn Djubayr, Ibn Batuta, and Ibn Fadhlan's account of the Bulgarians never fail to surprise us with their wealth of observation. The explanations they offer, however, are weak and, whether factual or magical, fall short of consistent rationality and, still more, of scientific rigor. The key to the ethnological enterprise is the discovery of a strange new world and the concomitant effort to overcome this strangeness through rational discourse. But along with this viewpoint goes a sense of superiority. Difference and superiority make up the objective essence of what ethnology aims at, even with the addition of understanding and sympathy.

Beginning in the seventeenth century, the marked distance separating Islam and Europe enabled European travelers—and they were legion—to practice (unconsciously) a kind of Islamic ethnology. And we have pointed out, apropos of the eighteenth century and especially of the Romantic vision of Islam, the presence in various European works of distinctly ethnological intuitions and intentions.

Modern ethnological study of Islam claims to be scientific to the extent that it invokes, among other things, strictly defined categories. But it remains (like Orientalism with respect to history) a marginal branch of European and American ethnology, unoriginal and backward, forever lagging behind the conceptual and methodological advances of that discipline.[29] In the case of the French ethnological school of North Africa we find in addition the malevolence and doctrinaire assumptions denounced by Fanon.[30] The ethnopsychiatric school of Algiers dehistoricizes and primitivizes the Arab—there is no denying the intimate, perhaps unconscious, link between this supposed science and the contemptuous attitude of the colonialist. And, conversely, there was a sharp about-face among students of Arab-Berber ethnology the moment that the Arabs began to free themselves from the yoke of colonialism: condescension turned into sympathy, respect, at times even mythic glorification. The changing fashions in Western study of Islam have made it clear to me how dependent scholars are on the *Zeitgeist* and even more on the strengths and weaknesses of the society around them. The mind ought to be free, and the search for truth ought to be above the contingencies of politics.

One French ethnologist of the classic school, a man whose research interests lay outside of Islam, did write some striking pages on the spirit and destiny of Islam. But Lévi-Strauss's reflections on this subject, though they draw upon his experience as an ethnologist and often amount to ethnological impressionism, are essentially philosophical in nature.[31]

Lévi-Strauss was concerned above all with Islamic India, and his discourse begins with its art. In Muslim art, he tells us, we can trace no organic connection between the parts and the whole: it compensates for its archictectural poverty with the splendor of its materials. "Why did Moslem art collapse so completely once it had passed its peak? It went from the palace to the bazaar without any transitional phase. This must have been a result of the rejection of images. Being deprived of all that Islam, a supremely communal religion, does not know what to make of solitude, just as Islamic civilization has always presented the paradoxical combination of the highest refinement with a certain "rustic" simplicity in its mores.

Lévi-Strauss then embarks on a long treatment of the spirit of Islam. Though short on information and patently hostile and unfair, this meditation remains astonishingly profound and intuitive. Islam is based on exclusion—barring women from the community of men and barring infidels from the community of the faithful. Hence the well-known tolerance of Muslims represents a "perpetual victory over themselves" and in the final analysis a pseudo-tolerance. Furthermore Islam creates anxiety in the minds of believers (although it promotes an aptitude for the active life) and thrives on casuistry. Islamic fraternity "rests on a cultural and religious basis. It has no economic or social contact with reality, the artist perpetuates a convention which is so anemic that it can be neither rejuvenated nor refertilized. Either it is sustained by gold or it collapses completely. At Lahore, the scholar who accompanied me had nothing but contempt for the Sikh frescoes which adorned the fort . . . and no doubt they were a far cry from the fantastic ceiling of mirrors in the Shish Mahal which sparkles like a star-studded sky. But as is so often the case when one compares contemporary India with Islam, they were vulgar, ostentatious, folk-like and charming."[32]

Speaking of the tombs and mausoleums, Lévi-Strauss is struck by the contrast between the vast dimensions, the richness of the exterior, and the cramped quarters housing the dead: "In Islam, the tomb divides up into a splendid monument, from which the dead man cannot benefit, and a niggardly abode . . . in which the deceased seems to be imprisoned."[33] The point is

character." Fundamentally hypocritical, it perpetuates the most
glaring inequalities.

Islam is further described as a "barrack-room religion,"
whence its characteristic homosexual promiscuity and the
fiercely masculine virtues associated with the Arab soul. These
virtues, however—jealousy, pride, heroism—are primarily
ways of compensating for a sense of inferiority before the Other,
the outsider, who is the great fissure in the Muslim personality
and its besetting terror. "This great religion is based not so
much on revealed truth as on an inability to establish links with
the outside world. In contrast to the universal kindliness of
Buddhism, or the Christian desire for dialogue, Moslem intolerance takes an unconscious form among those who are guilty of
it; although they do not always seek to make others share their
truth by brutal coercion, they are nevertheless (and this is more
serious) incapable of tolerating the existence of others as others.
The only means they have of protecting themselves against
doubt and humiliation is the 'negativation' of others, considered as witnesses to a different faith and a different way of
life."[34]

From the standpoint of world history, Islam appears as the
force that interposed itself between the Greek Mediterranean
West and the Buddhist East, both of which are rooted in the
same soil, the same immemorial culture, of the Indo-Euro-
peans. Greek influence began to be felt in the ancient land of
Bactria with the conquests of Alexander the Great. A number of
symbioses—which were also something like rediscoveries—
were taking shape and gave promise of restoring the unity of
man within a delicate and balanced culture, when the hurricane
of Islam swept down on them.

From the standpoint of religion, Islam, although the latest
religious form to evolve, marks a regression from the two universal forms that preceded it, Buddhism and Christianity, perhaps because it saw the light of day among a more backward
fraction of humanity. Of the three religions the first is the most

spiritual. "Over intervals of approximately five hundred years
mankind originated in turn Buddhism, Christianity, and Islam;
it is a striking fact that each stage, far from constituting an
advance on the previous one, should be seen rather as a regression. . . . Man never creates anything truly great except at the
beginning."[35]

Islam's very existence is intrusive: it split in two a world that
seemed destined to become one, thrusting itself between Hellenism and the Orient, between Christianity and Buddhism. It
Islamicized the West, preventing Christianity from growing
deeper and taking fuller possession of itself, which is what a
slow assimilation to Buddhism would have made possible. The
West became Muslim; that is, it became virile, powerful, war-
like, intellectual, preoccupied with organization, and lost its
chance of "remaining female."

A comparison between the Muslim art of India and both
Buddhist and non-Buddhist Oriental art thus leads up to a psy-
choanalytic anthropology and concludes in a philosophy of history. Unless of course Lévi-Strauss is really starting out from a
predetermined view of historical evolution that casts a long
shadow over his specific remarks, what he has to say about art is
not entirely unfounded. It is quite true, for example, that Islam
has a precisely defined notion of funerary art, which relates,
however, not to a concept of society and man (one that leaves it
baffled by solitude) but to a vision of death. A religion that
preaches the resurrection of the body, which in a way thinks of
death as a sleepy intermission between two lives, paradoxically
considers the corpse an insignificant envelope, a material husk
unrelated to the being who once inhabited it. So the comfort or
discomfort of the deceased is irrelevant. And yet, from the first
century of the Hijra on, there is a great deal of evidence concerning the obsession Muslims felt about tombs, their constricted
space, and the anxiety they create.[36]

On the strength of his impressions of Mughal art, Lévi-
Strauss ventures the generalization that Islamic art is overbur-

dened and highly unarchitectural. But it is precisely because
Islam has forbidden representation—which is, unquestionably,
an impoverishment—that Islamic art has established itself as
supremely architectural, not grandiose and pompous, but truly
great in that it expresses a passionate abstract piety on the
religious level and a powerful ambition on the historical level.
Lévi-Strauss says not a word about the grandeur of Islamic
architecture. He alludes to it only to belittle it by comparison
with a "folk-like and charming" Indian art. If he happens to
admire Islamic art, he obviously does not like it. And he does
not like it because the spirit of the Islamic civilization it reflects
with such narrow fidelity is repugnant to his ideals and tastes.
In reading Lévi-Strauss one realizes just how deep is the chasm
that separates, and perhaps will always separate, the Islamic
mind from certain regions of Western thought and sensibility.

Without question the malaise felt by Lévi-Strauss takes us
straight back to the old Western line of thinking about Islam.
This twentieth-century philosophe sees empty mosques, meets
traditional men of learning, traces the vestiges of history and,
trying to enliven a world that lay defenseless before him, he
populates it with the nightmares of Western tradition and dis-
joints it with his idea of an aborted historical opportunity.

Still, that malaise is keenly intuitive, and it catches sight of
some presumed truths.[37] Though Islam does not exclude wom-
en from social life, as Lévi-Strauss says, it has imposed heavy
chains on them and institutionalized their state of servitude
(something not unheard of, even in the West). But women in
Islamic society have always displayed less religious fervor than
men, together with a dynamic, subtle, and intense desire to
interact with the outside world.

The second point that deserves our attention in Lévi-
Strauss's description of Islam is his notion of structural intolerance. There, too, some objections need to be registered.
Comparatively speaking, Islam has shown a singular degree of
tolerance, but the French ethnologist was struck by the example

of Pakistan, a country that was specifically created out of the awareness by Muslims of their difference and superiority. This is hardly a typical case. In reality, Islam has long been a minority religion in so-called Islamic society. One might almost say that its weakness has come from having lived with others, surrounded by non-Muslims, and for too long, whereas from the Frankish period onward the West became religiously homogeneous. Internal schism can be quite productive in a monolithic culture, by promoting freedom of conscience, but it has to have a certain initial homogeneity to work with. Because it closed itself to those outside its confines, the West began to break up into conflicting parts, thereby acknowledging the existence of the other. Conversely, it is because Islam invented tolerance, and allowed active, threatening foreign bodies to lodge permanently in its midst that it had to defend itself and so closed ranks in self-affirmation against others. In Islam, as in the Arab-Islamic personality, the temptation and the menace of dissolution have always been just as important as the force of affirmation.

Still, as the ultimate revealed religion and as a religion of salvation—precisely because it claims to explain, acknowledge, and surpass earlier revelations—Islamic religion contains within itself an exclusionary, totalitarian principle. So does Christianity, even more so perhaps, though for different reasons, because Christian consciousness is animated by a feeling of peculiar legitimacy, of superiority, and antiquity. But that consciousness was shaken by the modern spirit and ultimately succumbed to it. And Islam has remained bound up with a kind of selfhood where the totality of the person is not recognized, where a man is not human except insofar as he is a believer.

That is why Lévi-Strauss's impressions are accurate and his explanations false.[38] Until very recent times, Islam would not admit the full humanity of any people except its own followers, so as to deny their right to spiritual freedom and autonomy of conscience (one could enter Islam, but not leave it). Conversely, it denied the humanity of others so as to acknowledge their freedom. Hence, intolerance and exclusion, far from being synonymous, were contraries. Intolerance was internal, it applied to the member of the community who was recognized as wholly human but not free; exclusion was external, it applied to others who were rejected but granted their freedom.

Lévi-Strauss ends up with what is for all practical purposes the *nature* of Islam, or at least the nature of its peculiar tendencies, frozen for all time. Islam fixed and eternal is contrasted with an equally eternal Buddhism and Christianity. Here Lévi-Strauss is unconsciously echoing old ideas that date from the Middle Ages. Born from the flames of battle and spread by the violent expansion of a desert people, Islam supposedly contained the seeds of aggression and exclusion. Its history, says Lévi-Strauss, is simply the development of this intrinsic fundamental structure.

But is it reasonable to believe that Islam bears the mark, like Cain, of some original sin? No doubt one could find something along this line in the Qur'an and, generally speaking, in the original context of Islam (e.g., the idea of the community, or *umma*). But the primitive Islamic community did not so much exclude the outside world as make an appeal to it. There was a permanent openness to the "infidels." Furthermore the Arab conquest was an essentially secular phenomenon, exclusive the way any ordinary imperialistic domination might be, not in the sense of a messianic movement. In the first two centuries after the Hijra, conversion of native peoples to the religion of the invaders proceeded slowly, and in the following three centuries it took place spontaneously. The spirit of the *jihad*, in the final analysis, is only a military fiction, a source of energy and enthusiasm at the outset, an ideal mobilization of defensive reflexes in the second Islamic period. A recent study points out how hard it was to rekindle the old fire of the jihad during the Crusades.[39] It remains true, however, that Islam contains a powerful element of autonomy and affirmation that cannot be adequately accounted for simply by the particular historical circumstances in which it is manifested. It is always there, beneath the surface, but it has to be concretely realized in history.

For Islam came onto the scene during a period when civilization bore the stamp of religious ideology, which in turn erected and informed a model of human selfhood. This age of ideology was characterized by a sort of truncated universality. Neither Hellenic culture nor Roman citizenship had opened the doors of their sanctuaries to all comers. For their part, Christianity and Islam rose to a total and immediate universality held together by God alone. But then exclusion inevitably became the dark side of this intense communion and concrete universal vision. Islam today continues to live by this age-old pattern, whereas Christianity, which is six centuries older, has twice undergone reform, in the sixteenth century, and again in the nineteenth, first on its own, then under pressure from the outside. Islam has yet to have an authentic reformation—it has been waiting for and badly needs one. But on one point Lévi-Strauss has made a trenchant observation: the fact that Islam is young as world religions go and that it was ahead of its time has led to its subsequent rigidity, because the revolutionary impulse always engenders the temptation to conservatism, and the idea of perfection stymies efforts at improvement.

Lévi-Strauss's intuitions in the matter of Islamic art and psychology are as striking in their broad grasp of the truth as his treatment of the philosophy is arbitrary and unsatisfactory. Its subjectivism is glaringly self-indulgent, mental constructs turn into flights of fancy, and history is manipulated and subordinated to generous but inconsistent ideals. The *Ewig-weibliche* is exalted as the principle of supreme goodness, and Buddhism is likewise magnified for having actualized it. In his quest for the meaning of history, Lévi-Strauss shows how much he lacks a feeling for history: Buddhism and Christianity would never have come together. He has injected as much Hellenism into the East as he possibly could. Islam did not cut the world in half.

Quite the contrary, its role as a connecting link between the great centers of civilization and the fringes of the Orient is a well-established fact.

Both as a religion and as a human achievement, Islam rises above the *primitivism*, however benevolent, of Buddhism:[40] it is the religion that comes closest to reason. For the Beyond is not just a source of terror, it is the guarantee of morality, and the line of demarcation between good and evil. Besides, the universality of Buddhism is abstract, it never meshes with the real world, and it makes no allowances for the violence of man and of history. In our time we may legitimately reflect on and admire it (and its message is quite admirable), but that is because we have centuries of Christianity, Islam, and humanism behind us. Each one of humanity's great religions represents one form of human experience. As such they all necessarily amputate the person in one way or another, they close off a vast range of possibilities— a restrictiveness scarcely compensated for by whatever inherent flexibility the person may have. There are values that Islam has missed, not that it totally denied them, it simply failed to cultivate them. The same is true of other world religions: each is the repository of a sacred message, enveloped in concrete forms, all of which cut off and limit evolutionary processes, various noble tendencies in human beings, this or that color in the immense rainbow of truth. But these religions have a past and a present, they have left their traces on the matrix of history—that is, on human consciousness.

The task facing the Arab-Islamic mind today is at once to preserve the genius of Islam and to make some corrections in the course it has taken. Islam remains above all, as Hegel said, the purest, the most abstract and transcendent love of the One ever seen. For those ravaged by the violence of life it offers a tranquil return to God, the peace that its name implies. This is the irreducible core of Islam, and any attempt to Christianize or Buddhicize it would be to dilute it with an eye to destroying it completely. But a sharper accent could be placed on the theme of mercy, which is the specifically Islamic dimension of charity. Humanity will never become an expanded version of the *umma*, as Muslims once hoped and dreamed. It is pluralistic, and this pluralism must be accepted, the singularity of its component parts must be honored—something that has already occurred in the turbulent depths of the contemporary Islamic mind.

# 4

# Islam and German Thought[1]

## GERMANIC-ARAB RELATIONS

In the Middle Ages, it seems, Germanic-Islamic relations were not governed by pure politics, but marched to the rhythm of cultural and spiritual concerns. Frederick Hohenstaufen was the prototypical source of a certain kind of sympathetic German response to Islam, and the precursor of all intelligent Western Islamophiles. As the head of Christendom, he fought against the political power of Islam while openly admiring Muslim valor. Yet he did not stop there: Islam for him meant a world of peace, of art, and the delicate enjoyment of life. So this was no encounter between the usual sort of Germanic warrior and the military fervor of Islam.

In Sicily, that extraordinary rendezvous point and locus of syncretism or even fusion between two civilizations, the freest minds on both sides longed to break the religious and cultural shackles restraining humanity's upward surge. Renan describes Frederick correctly and perspicaciously as a great man whose "leading idea . . . was *civilization* in the most modern sense of the word."[2] Frederick II made the most of Arab thought, which was more advanced than that of his Christian contemporaries, as well as of the refinements of Islamic civilization. Clearly superior to the world about him, he struggled, pondered, loved, and gave free rein to his sensuality.

But after the splendid adventure of the Hohenstaufen (Frederick and Manfred, in particular), the German mind turned in upon itself, breaking off all exchanges with Islam. In the modern period, with the exception of Austria, which was the front line of resistance to Turkish assaults, the German-speaking world, badly fragmented, lacking a concerted diplomacy, and commercially linked to the North, did not experience the continual trafficking, the struggles, and the permanent contacts that France, Spain, Italy, and England had with Islam in the Mediterranean basin or Asia.

And in the nineteenth century, when modern Germany was emerging and then realizing its destiny as a nation-state, it did not follow the colonialist pattern of most great European countries, doubtlessly because it was absorbed in the task of organizing its internal forces. Though convinced of its genius and bursting with a sense of its power, Germany could neither spread its language and culture across the world nor, in the final analysis, go beyond the confines of Europe. Bismarck failed to get Germany to play an international role, as France and England had. In retrospect, it is obvious that this failure to acquire colonies prevented Germany from leaving its mark on large portions of humanity. All the seeds of its cultural and intellectual life were sown in Europe,[3] especially France, and it was through France that as an Arab and native of the Maghrib, I came to know and admire German philosophy. In the same way, Germany unleashed all its explosive political power on the European continent. As the rest of the world looked on, it played its historic role in a drama of pain, violence, and madness, thereby hastening the eclipse of Europe.

Germany rediscovered Islam after Bismarck, during the reign of Wilhelm II, but apart from any colonialist context.[4] Frederick Hohenstaufen's plans for cultural intercourse gave way to political relations, to the game of alliance-building—in a word, to something based on a pre-established distance between both parties. The alliance with Turkey was the zenith of this sort of rapprochement, which turned out to be radically different from the colonialist intrusion into the heart of another's territory. In the case of German policy, there was neither intimacy nor hostility but a positive inclination, a favorable prejudice. Germany had no record of aggression against Islam, had not founded colonies on Arab or Muslim soil; it was the enemy of Islam's enemies. In short, it was an ally of Turkey, which for many reasons still stood for something in the Arab-Islamic mind.

In a situation in which the political and historical tides were flowing against Turkey, however—as was the case with Arabia and the Fertile Crescent which, as late as 1914, found themselves under the Turkish yoke after they had broken free of England's grasp—the positions were to be virtually reversed. The Arab revolt led by Husayn ibn Ali was thus pro-English, anti-Turkish, and anti-German, even if it was only chance that made him the de facto enemy of Germany. Contrariwise, the Maghrib, which was officially aligned with France, was sentimentally on the side of Turkey and so of Germany as well, but here too the relationship with Germany was indirect, a sort of logical repercussion.

So the flimsy ties binding Germany to the Islamic and, in particular, to the Arabic-speaking world were the creatures of pure political contingency. Despite the generally warm atmosphere in which they were conducted and despite the absence of handicaps from a colonial past, German-Arab relations remained abstract, they had no existential density. But, both before and after 1914, the Mashriq and the Maghrib were essentially oriented toward France and England, whether to serve them, to fight against them, or to be influenced by their cultures. And when, at the turn of the century, great thinkers like Shaykh Muhammad Abduh reflected on the destiny of Islam or the Arab world, they always related it to those two great powers. Abduh thought that France was Islam's real enemy and that its brand of colonialism tended to destroy the Islamic personality. England, in his view, was more flexible: its aims in planting colonies were economic and posed less of a threat to the culture and vitals, so to speak, of the country in question.[5] Abduh's comparison disregarded Germany, logically enough, since it had played no active part in the evolution of Arab history.

World War II brought Germany abruptly to the forefront of Arab concerns and posed a moral dilemma for Arabs. Hitler attacked the Jews but he had nothing against the Arabs, politically speaking at least. His strategy even called for their support and friendship. Besides, Arabs might well have considered that a German victory would necessarily have spelled the end of the Jewish homeland in Palestine and the liberation of Arab territories under French and English domination. So it is not surprising that Arab leaders hesitated about what attitude to adopt toward Germany, once again the virtual ally of the Arab cause. Some of them, such as the Mufti of Jerusalem, went over to the Nazis. Others were happy to see the authority of the colonial powers weak and in disarray. In a few cases they even tried, with direct help from the Germans or by exploiting German advances in North Africa, to free themselves from colonialist control. Germanophile Arabs did, however, restrict their view of the war, for which their own countries served as a battleground, to the perspective of their local struggles and interests. Thus Morocco, Egypt, and Tunisia merely made timid efforts to wrest a few concessions from the Allies. But that was scarcely threatening, since we can imagine today—and back then a man like Churchill was well aware of this—what a catastrophe a general revolt in Egypt and the Maghrib would have been for the Allied strategy in Africa. (There was, in fact, a revolt in Iraq, led by Rashid Ali al-Jaylani.)

What must not be forgotten here is that Arab leaders with a broad following came down on the side of the Allies, whether out of conviction or calculation. The most farsighted among them—Nahhas in Egypt, Thaalbi and Bourguiba in Tunisia—looked beyond the horizons of their native lands, realized what was at stake in this worldwide conflict, and foresaw the eventual crushing defeat of Germany. Nahhas and Thaalbi put their faith in England's unshakable tenacity, while Bourguiba, to some extent, believed in the values of democracy and for tactical reasons advised betting on the Allies.

On the whole the positions taken by Arab leaders reveal a certain divergence, with a majority ultimately favoring the Allies.[6] The masses, however, preponderantly favored a German victory, through which they hoped to be freed from colonialist rule. Beyond that, Nazism fueled the anti-Semitism that undeniably smoldered among the common people—who had no idea of the scope of Nazi persecution or of the dreadful atrocities being committed in Europe. Their anti-Semitism was naive, instinctive, fitful, and they would have condemned all the refinements of Nazi cruelty, its grim mixture of technology and pathology. Lastly, it is true that as a group Arabs admired German courage, daring, and know-how; they were impressed by the way Germans fought almost single-handedly against a gigantic coalition of enemies. But here, too, things were not clear-cut since the Tunisians, for example, were united in their fear and disapproval of a possible Italian takeover, which they felt would be an intolerable humiliation.

Apart from the political accidents marking a century of common history, one wonders if there are any deeper bonds between Islam and German civilization. Might there be some sort of affinity between the Germanic and Islamic mind, as in Lévi-Strauss's observation on "those two, sociologically remarkable, species, the Germanophile Moslem and the Islamicized German"?[7] Pan-Germanism has already been compared only too often to pan-Arabism; Nasser has been likened to Hitler; and the Ba'ath party has been traced back to Rosenberg's Nazi ideology. One thing is certain: if the Arabs are ill informed about German culture, the Germans have shown a special inclination to understand and appreciate Islam. I have already touched on the valuable contribution made by German Orientalism to the understanding of Islamic religion and culture, and I shall shortly discuss the vision of Islam in Hegel and Spengler. But outside the world of books, what was the actual situation?

The truth is that the Germans, living so far away from Islamic nations and neither struggling against them nor competing with them on their own territory, have thought highly of Islam and some of them have even personally embraced it. Generally speaking, the inhabitants of northern Europe, including the Anglo-Saxons, have felt a stronger attraction to Islam than the Latins. If someone like T. E. Lawrence would be hard to conceive of in France, he would be utterly unthinkable in

Italy. Conversely, traditional Muslim Arabs have admired Germany and England much more than France. Shawqi praises English "virtue" as akin to classic Islamic ideals.[8] Likewise, German tradition and Germanic discipline have been warmly received by some very conservative Islamic thinkers. The Turk Talaat Pasha lived in Germany between the two world wars, and the Tunisian Bash Hamba was buried in Berlin. In addition many tradition-minded Arab leaders, such as Abduh in Egypt and Thaalbi in Tunisia, were secret Anglophiles. In contrast, France, with its intellectual universalism, attracted only "liberal" intellectuals like Taha-Hussein or members of the Europeanized bourgeoisie, not authentic representatives of Islam.

With regard to the structures of Germanic and Islamic civilizations, certain critics have had little difficulty finding supposedly common features such as militarism, a conquest mentality, the cult of force and collective vitality, and so on. But which Germany and which Islam are we talking about? In point of fact, the Prussian spirit is the antithesis of both the Islamic spirit and the Arab mind. And the systematic approach of German thinking is utterly foreign to contemporary Arab intellectual life, which evinces no feelings of metaphysical anxiety or strivings to reach inaccessible spiritual realms, but displays a robust rationality, pragmatism, and a keen sense of politics.

From the standpoint of current history, however, there are some striking similarities to be noted here: just like the Arab world, the Germanic world has suffered from a painful split between external reality and inner feelings of value and greatness. This had led to a constant state of agitation, an emotional turbulence, and a whole pattern of compensatory behavior that can be compared with the upheavals in the Arab world over the past 100 years. Until quite recently the German character could be described by two contradictory features: on the one hand, youth and enthusiasm and, on the other, the persistence of traditional ideals and social and political structures. This same dichotomy can be found appearing, after a certain lapse of time, in Arab culture today.

## HEGEL

What German thinkers admired about Islam was its self-projection or in other words, its historical double image: the youth and enthusiasm of Arab life in the first century of the Hijra together with Islam's affirmation of itself down through the ages as an irreducible autonomous structure and a perennially combative force. This image has been handed down to us by two philosophers of history who worked at a century's remove from each other, Hegel in the early 1800s, and Oswald Spengler in the early 1900s.

The Hegel who took an interest in Islam was not the young man who wrote the *Phenomenology of Mind* and numerous other works on the philosophy of religion, but the later Hegel, the author of the incomparable *Lectures on the Philosophy of History*. The amount of space he devotes to Islam in this work is minimal: a few scattered notes when the context calls for them and one long passage of four pages in the fourth and last part of the work, which deals with the Germanic world. But the vision contained in these four pages is striking—both profoundly true and remarkably poetic, the most perceptive account by a European up till that time.

Starting in his Introduction, Hegel describes the Germanic world as the "fourth moment of universal history."[9] Its destiny begins under the sign of a gigantic antithesis between the spiritual principle of Christianity and the secular reality of barbarism. "All that is secular is consequently given over to rudeness and capricious violence. The Mohammedan principle—the enlightenment of the Oriental world—is the first to contravene this barbarism and caprice."

Later on, when Hegel deals directly with the problem of Mohammedanism,[10] he presents it as the *Revolution of the Orient*, "which destroyed all particularity and dependence, and perfectly cleared up and purified the soul . . . making the abstract One the absolute object of attention, and to the same extent, pure subjective consciousness—the knowledge of this One alone—the only aim of reality."[11]

Islam, then, sprang full-blown onto the stage of history with an immediate, luminous force. It transcended the negativ-

ity of the Oriental mind, as expressed in the slavish subjection
of Mind, and equally transcended the particularity of the Jewish
God, instantly taking the high ground of universality, thereby
purifying and liberating human intelligence. "The worship of
the One is the only final aim of Mahometanism."[12]

But this One is abstract, even though it exercises a determining power over the mind. It is not concrete like the Christian
God who incarnates the divine in human form. Hegel stresses
the clarity, simplicity, and universal relevance of the Islamic
principle. The abstract nature of Islam, however, its most salient feature, is accompanied by a tremendous enthusiasm.
Muslim fanaticism is, properly speaking, enthusiasm for an
abstract reality which bears "only a desolating, destructive
relation to the concrete; but that of Mahometanism was, at the
same time, capable of the greatest elevation—an elevation free
from all petty interests, and united with all the virtues that
appertain to magnanimity and valor."[13]

That poetic description gives rise to a coherent vision of
Islam as a historical movement. On the cultural level, Islam, as
Hegel sees it, has always busied itself with God and with God
alone. It is basically oriented toward the transcendent world as
the privileged object of knowledge, and not toward the historical or natural world. Science has the honor of fastening
itself upon the sacred, whereas in Europe, a major shift of
attention has fixed all intellectual energies on the task of
knowing the world. On the political level, Hegel sees the lack
of a stable pattern of succession as the great flaw of the Islamic
system.

Hegel is aware of Islam's historical decadence, though he
has no solid explanation to offer for it. But the parallel with
Europe remains implicit in his thought. Europe owes its rise to
power as much to a valid original principle as to its dialectical
might, which provided the foundation of its development. This
is evidently an inward-looking thesis, and makes no allowances
for a dialectic between civilizations or for outside intervention.
It is on this latter point that I should like to shed some light.

The extraordinary paradox of Western European history is
that its civilization, one of the loftiest and richest ever known

(and the apex of universal history), sprang up amid rampant barbarism, in a human and cultural void, and from a kind of inorganic, unorganized medium. It was the result of a dialectic carried to its final extreme. The collapse of the State in the Middle Ages cleared the way for the emergence of the rational State, the reign of feudalism did the same for democracy, oppression by the Church led to freedom of conscience, and the bloodiest national antagonisms brought forth the nation as an agency promoting human and cultural development. In the seventh century Islam got off to a flying start and seemed to hold out the promise of raising humanity to new evolutionary heights, but it was not destined to lead history down the traumatic path to modernity. It fell to those parts of Europe which the Roman Empire forgot (Gaul and England) and the parts lying beyond the pale (Germany), repeatedly invaded and overrun, shaken by violence and torn asunder, to attack the formidable task, not, as Hegel thought, of bringing history to a close, but of guiding it on a critical step forward, of prompting a unique advance.

Europe stepped out of the darkness by denying and going beyond itself, but that was not enough. Its working principles had to have a certain intrinsic fertility and the capacity for self-transcendence. As opposed to this confusing identity crisis, this long groping quest (because the European principle was at once so fecund and so indecisive), Islam offers a different model of cultural development. But its very success, the degree to which it met the needs of its time, served to imprison it in a relative immobility. In spite of its "barbarous" novelty, Arab culture was too far along in its evolution to imitate its Germanic counterpart and passively welcome influences from a foreign world. It was driven to establish itself as a grand normative principle and, once having given birth to Islam, it was practically condemned to constant active creativity, hence to a sort of indestructibility. It would be a self-affirming power, not a dialectical movement. Meanwhile Europe was drifting into the chaotic freedom of historical dynamism.

The Middle East, the environment where Islam found a

home, was already an old and tired world, though it had a superior material culture. And contrary to what Hegel thought, Europe did not pull itself up by its own bootstraps: external forces played a part, and no small one, in its development—the ancient East, to begin with, along with Islam and, above all, Greco-Roman antiquity. For Germanic culture was only a form of energy—that was the key to its vital contribution; that is, in its youth and its explosive effect on the decrepit structures of the past, not because of any positive qualities inherent in the freedom-loving Germanic soul, which is rather one of the narcissistic illusions propagated by nineteenth-century German thinkers.

The phenomenon of Europe was self-created, but its true essence could not have flowered without the mediation of classical antiquity. On this point both Hegel and Spengler seem to have missed the historical truth. Perhaps they were misled by their keen awareness that the exemplary character of antiquity was a fiction and that, on the contrary, Europe's awakening was quite authentic. Yet antiquity had already provided the Carolingian renaissance with the cultural content without which all those new energies would have spun in the void, a content that (however distorted) gave life to the medieval period.

To correct this distortion the Renaissance (less important than the Reformation but completely ignored by Hegel)[14] offered a more authentic return to antiquity, something more than a dressed up, made up, misrepresentation of something radically heterogeneous. Ultimately, with the coming of the French Revolution, antiquity became a kind of painted backdrop to the real action, but even then the potent ideas of liberty, democracy, and republican government, though they were the legitimate offspring of their day and age, nonetheless were somewhat indebted to the ancient world.

But Islam had no such antiquity, no source of mediation and established standards. Hellenism remained foreign to it, while the ancient Orient, whether Mesopotamian or Sasanid, could supply no more than models of governmental and economic organization. Furthermore the prodigious success that Islam experienced gave it a classical status by the eleventh century, and since it had been, as Hegel noted, the great Revolution of the East, its archaic phase constituted what might be called the modernity of the Orient. Thus the history of Islam flowed to a pounding, exhausting rhythm and in complete solitude. When it struggled to find new life, it had nowhere to look for support against itself but from within or from its Arab supporters. In Islam, therefore, internal structures predominate over external ones, since there is no other historical locus that can also serve as home.

The effort to return to historical roots took place within Islam itself—split between Islam as a heroic, sacred realm and Islam as classicism in full flower—and the nineteenth-century *Nahda* arose precisely in order to frame that past in "some other place" without first undergoing any schism, alienation, or differentiation other than that of temporal distance. Islam appears to have lived a parasitic existence, and many Orientalists have taken a malicious pleasure in underlining its "lack of originality," but the core of the problem lies deeper than appearances would suggest.

Relations with the outside world in this case cannot be measured by cultural or technical borrowings: they are located rather in that intimate region that is the heart of a people's dialectical history. This points the way toward the corrections and expansions that must be made in Hegel's vision. The European dialectic is first and foremost internal, but it depends upon links with a world beyond its borders: a world of the past (antiquity) and of the present (Islam). That is true not so much because Islam served as a vehicle for the Greek heritage but because it destroyed, devalued, or absorbed Eastern Christianity and in so doing made Europe the true homeland of that religion, just as it became the true heir of classical antiquity. As for Islam itself, its development did not essentially follow a dialectical pattern or at least this dialectic produced no tangible results—until the present day.

## OSWALD SPENGLER

Written a century after the *Lectures on the Philosophy of History*, Spengler's *Decline of the West* deals at length with the theme of Arab culture.[15]

Spengler rejects any notion of a progressive spirit coming to breathe life into the various forms of civilization, binding them to one another in a common enterprise. Although Hegel allots an important place to the Orient, he spends only a few pages on Islam which, by the way, he detaches from its Oriental context and inserts into the medieval period like a foreign body, like a splendid flowering that withered—in a word, like a marginal element in universal history. Spengler, in contrast, considers Islam the central phenomenon of Oriental history, which he observes from a totally different angle. A third and crucial difference here is that Hegel practically excludes all non-European civilizations from the advance of Mind, whereas Spengler repudiates all forms of Eurocentrism, and reduces the history of the West to the normal proportions of the history of one great culture among others. Both philosophers, however, implicitly agree that History is approaching its consummation.

As his French translator noted (an opinion later echoed by Muhammad Iqbal)[16] Spengler's fundamental intuition involves the discontinuity and incommunicability of the various cultures. We shall be looking successively at the foundations of these cultures, at the *pseudomorphosis* or alienation of Arab culture and, finally, at the decline of Western culture and its metamorphosis into civilization, three central themes in Spengler's thought.


1.  Among the eight cultures whose course Spengler charts there are three that stand apart from the rest and make up the core of world history: ancient, Arabian, and Western, or Apollinian, Magian, and Faustian—terms borrowed from Goethe, but with strong Nietzschean overtones. What makes a culture live, what drives it (and all its material elements) forward and thus distinguishes it from other cultures is the central aim it has in view.

The Apollinian Culture recognized as actual only that which was immediately present in time and place—and thus it repudiated the background as pictorial element. The Faustian strove through all sensuous barriers towards infinity—and it projected the centre of gravity of the pictorial idea into the distance by means of perspective. The Magian felt all happening as an expression of mysterious powers that filled the world-cavern with their spiritual substance.

The symbols that sustained the Magian soul are, he writes, "Alchemy and Kabbala, the Philosophers' Stone, the Holy Scriptures, the Arabesque, the inner form of the tale of the 'Thousand and One Nights.' "[17]

Each of these cultures is circumscribed in time and space, but according to norms totally different from those laid down by traditional historiography. Spengler shatters conventional periodization so as to uncover and identify, beneath the seemingly clear surface of a historical datum, the true organic features of a culture that make it sui generis. He argues that ancient Greco-Roman culture first saw the light about 1100 B.C. by the Aegean Sea, and that its typical representative was Homer or later Pythagoras. Western culture became aware of itself and of its peculiar genius near the end of the first millennium A.D. The West was the homeland of Gothic architecture, of farms reclaimed from the wilderness, of Cistercian monks, and the heroes of the Germanic forest. It was at this time that its Christianity, as profoundly different from primitive Oriental Christianity as Saint Bernard was from Saint Paul, found its truth, which is the historical truth of Christianity.

Spengler equates Magian culture with Arab culture, but he stretches the notion of Arabness too far in time and space. This culture, he maintains, emerged as a distinctive structure about 500 B.C.;

And in the time of Augustus, in the countries between Nile and Tigris, Black Sea and South Arabia, there appears . . . the Magian soul of Arab Culture with its algebra, astrology, and alchemy, its mosaics and arabesques, its caliphates and mosques, and the sacraments and scriptures of the Persian, Jewish, Christian, "post-Classical" and Manichaean religions.[18]

The subject at issue here is thus not Arab culture as generally understood but rather an Arabian-Persian-Aramaean Middle East whose reality and personality are etched out against the ruins of the ancient Orient and whose geographical space will later coincide exactly with the Arab conquest. This Orient is the hearth and home of religious man, of religion as the summit of the mind, of the invisible world in its highest expression, hence of the category of Magian thinking. We can go along with Spengler's sensible idea that the same soil that nurtured Christ, the Talmud, and the Halakah also brought forth the rich harvest of Mazdak, Mani, and Muhammad. And it was in one and the same spiritual world that the Sunna and the Tafsir took root.

Spengler is in a way the poet of total authenticity, a thinker with extreme sensitivity to the in-depth, underlying truth of each culture. This is what led him to deny the existence of any dramatic progressive pattern in history and ultimately, by rejecting any kind of solidarity or commerce among civilizations, to lose all sense of universality and of ongoing change. We know that, among his other failings, Spengler's quest for authenticity—a badly misused word these days—led him into a fixation with the past, that is, with that stage of a society's evolution at which it coincided perfectly with itself. Thus in his eyes the real Russia would be Dostoevski's, not Tolstoy's—the land of the illiterate muzhik, not of Peter the Great and his transplanted Enlightenment. For Spengler the countryside, with its peasants, aristocrats, and old-time traditions, constitutes the true essence of society, the core than can only be betrayed by cosmopolitan cities, with their capitalism, socialism, and fallacious learning.

Insofar as each culture is closed in upon itself, incapable both of moving off to another realm and of undergoing the influence of a culture outside it, it is necessarily struck with paralysis, it experiences a basic alienation, every time a foreign culture worms its way into it or tries to impose its forms on it. This superimposition then turns into aggression or poisonous infiltration. And here Spengler develops his theory of the pseudomorphosis of "Arab" culture.

2. Pseudomorphosis takes place when a young culture tries to express itself but manages to do so only through the medium of borrowed foreign forms, which disfigure its soul and stifle its creative spirit. But that soul, though buried beneath the debris of a false expressiveness, stands ready to liberate itself at a moment's notice. More than any other culture, that of the "Arabs" between the third century B.C. and the appearance of Islam suffered from this entrapment of its inner genius in ancient forms.

Thanks to the philological prejudices of European historiography, the field of Arab culture was, strictly speaking, divided arbitrarily into the ancient period, the Greco-Roman period, and the Arab period. In fact, what is called the Oriental literature of late antiquity is a phase of Arab literature when it wore the mask of Greek expression. In the same way, Arab science began its career in the first centuries of the Christian era in Ctesiphon, Jundishapur, Sura, Edessa, and Nisibis; and it was this science, I might add, that would later develop with the Arabs, in the proper sense, and reach a widely acknowledged level of excellence.[19]

In more westerly areas, however, particularly in Alexandria, this flowering was ruined by pseudomorphosis. Finally, the authenticity I have spoken of, which was both servile and covertly self-possessed, is manifest in an art whose unity over an entire millennium makes such a striking impression upon us. The same mentality, in fact, presided over the building of Christian basilicas, Mazdaean temples, and Islamic mosques: a mentality dominated by the cosmic feeling of the crypt and inclined to use the dome as the expression of its magical experience. Thus "the oldest mosque is the Pantheon as rebuilt in the reign of Hadrian" by Syrian foremen. Similarly, when Islam transformed Hagia Sophia into a mosque, it was simply "taking back old property."

Hence the destiny of pre-Islamic Arab culture was a tragic destiny: denied the "fruits of its maturity" by pseudomorphosis, it went under at the very time (from the third to the fifth century A.D.) when it might have given birth to a classical age and reveled in its own splendor.

It was only in its late phase that Arab culture was saved and nursed back to health by Islam, which restored its vitality and enabled it to be itself again. The Islamic moment of Magian culture is therefore the process by which it was reconciled with itself after the trials of pseudomorphosis. This is why Spengler applies the term *Arab* to a historical totality that stretches far beyond the strict ethnological limits of the Arab world.

The greatness of the Arab phenomenon (in the narrower sense) and the Islamic phenomenon, which threw in its lot with the Arabs, arose from the fact that Islam freed Arab culture from its chains. Islam crashed like a lightning bolt into a domain whose inner structure had been waiting for something like this for centuries, in the impulsive thrust "of a soul that feels itself in a hurry, that notes in fear the first symptoms of old age before it has had youth. This emancipation of Magian mankind is without a parallel."[20]

This "fulguration" has the advantage of explaining many things, but by reinserting Islam into its broad historical environment Spengler destroys its originality. And he winds up in fact by affirming that Islam is merely "the Puritanism of the whole group of Early Magian religions"[21] and not a new religion, except insofar as one could apply that term to, say, Lutheranism. This is because Justinian, "the most fateful personality in Arab history," looked to Rome and not to his own Eastern milieu. By turning away from the Nestorians and Monophysites, Justinian allowed Islam to present itself as a new religion rather than as a puritanical current within Levantine Christianity. Spengler justly remarks that Islam, which came forth from Mecca, that little pocket of ancient paganism, cannot be considered a religion of the desert. Mecca was "a little island of ancient Arabian paganism in the midst of a world of Jews and Christians, a mere relic that had long been mined by the ideas of the great Magian religions."[22]

3. The third theme I shall analyze is that of the West and its decline. We have already seen that Spengler repudiated any sort of Eurocentrism. He explicitly says that his vision of history is Copernican, not Ptolemaic. Europe thus forfeits its exemplary

status, along with all its special privileges. Its historical role is
now an ordinary one. Its giant stature shrinks to normal proportions. It is subject to limitations in time and space. As for the
future of the West, it is simply "a particular historical event,
inevitably demarcated in its form and duration." The flowering
of Western culture lasted but a few hundred years and, beginning with Napoleon, it entered upon the stage of "civilization."

Culture is opposed to civilization as the inside is to the
outside, as the vigor of youth and maturity is to the decline of
old age. The first part of each dyad represents a project's greatness and creative élan, and draws its strength from an ardent,
aroused soul. The second part represents the dying fall, the
moment when external expressions no longer correspond to
anything within. European civilization displayed its imposing
exterior to the nineteenth century, but it was in vain: behind the
front of imperialism, industrialization, the reign of the great
metropolis, and the zenith of power, the inner creativity had
gone.[23] Great music, for example, or great painting will hence-
forth be out of the question. "The only things left to the West are
*extensive possibilities*."

As one great culture among many, European culture is
rooted in a given landscape and evolves within a specific framework, which is original and incommunicable. This notion of
Europe's particularity is fatally bound up with the idea that its
destiny is unexceptional. The history of the West no longer
contains a unique universality, and any hope of fusing the
human race into a universal society has to be rejected out of
hand. Finally, the decline of the West, which leads to death, has
already set in.

Putting aside its paradoxical features, Spengler's work
poses serious problems for contemporary thinkers. At this juncture, I should like to sketch out a critique of it.

Among his characterizations of various cultures, Spengler's
treatment of Arab (or Magian) culture is no doubt the least
convincing. Muhammad Iqbal has already cast aspersions on
the term *Magian*. "I don't deny," he writes, "that Islam has been
covered by a crust of magic. As a matter of fact, my main

purpose in giving these lectures has been to offer a view of the spirit of Islam with its overlying Magian strata removed, which, as I see it, have led Spengler astray. His ignorance of Muslim thought on the question of time, as well as the way in which the 'I,' as a free, autonomous center of experience, has found a place in the religious experience of Islam—that ignorance is absolutely astounding."[24]

Strictly speaking, the Semitic religions (and Islam more than any other) are strongly opposed to magic. Islam came into being in order to master the old anxieties, and its overall rationality cannot be doubted. But it is quite true that the contribution of the Orient to human spirituality all over the world has been made through religion; and it is through religion (which became their most salient characteristic) that the Arabs have made their way to civilization. Seen from this angle, Spengler's Magian theory has the merit of underlining the fact that Judaism, Christianity, and Islam all belong to the same spiritual homeland. Hence it is no longer possible to distinguish Judeo-Christian from Islamic tradition by conceiving the former as rational and the latter as fundamentally magical.

However debatable it may be, Spengler's exploration of that specific organism called Arab culture continues to provide the student of history with a good deal of food for thought. It sheds new light both on the renewal that swept over the East near the end of the first millennium B.C. and on a certain continuity that Islam, far from breaking, has vivified and consolidated. This Persian-Arab-Aramaean Orient reveals itself as sharply distinct from the earliest Eastern culture as well as from the Hellenistic culture which later invaded it. Christianity was born in this specific environment (which, before Spengler, scholars of antiquity had misunderstood), and so was Islam. It is true, for example, that for its dogmatic content Islamic tradition drew heavily upon Syro-Aramaean sources, and that after the Arab conquest the *Sunna* and the *Fiqh* borrowed still more from them. But, just as the Jewish Yahweh, while assuming many aspects of the Canaanite Baal, remains a peculiarly Jewish being, so the God of Islam, thoroughly Judeo-Christian as he was, remains

the Allah and Rahman of the Arabian Peninsula. Qur'anic legis-
lation, the *hajj*, the general tone of the Prophet's message are all
Arab. And later on the *Fiqh* would preserve some purely
Arabian ethnographic features, which constituted a foreign element in their Oriental milieu by the very fact that Arab identity
found itself on the fringe of the Orient, living as it did by a
spirituality that was irreducibly original.

At this point it makes sense to dwell briefly on the attractive
theory of pseudomorphosis. I would not challenge the idea that
the Orient resisted Greek influence, that it maintained its identity beneath a Hellenistic veneer. Despite the importance of the
Alexandrian school or the Syriac school of Jundishapur, Greek
thought failed to penetrate the deep creative core of the Oriental
soul. And the later renaissance of Hellenic studies under the
first Abbasids, which played such a crucial role in the emergence of Arab science and philosophy, and which also left its
mark on Muslim theology, dogma, and law, never touched any
vital nerve in that culture, and still less did it affect the internal
movement of Islamic civilization. In criticizing Becker, we have
seen how Hellenism was alien to Islam, and we can extend this
conclusion to cover the entire pre-Islamic East.

Islam accomplished what Persia, even under the Achae-
menids, was never able to do, namely, unify the Orient around a
spiritual and cultural tradition. In the seventh century A.D. the
Orient was suffering from an ideological and political void.
There was a profound need to establish an identity, but it had to
be connected to a spiritual aspiration that was lofty, new, and
open to the future; and this need was the key to Islam's success.
Islam did not deliver the Orient from the shackles of Spengler's
exaggerated pseudomorphosis (a notion that led him to make
statements as paradoxical as they were brilliant), but by filling
up the void, by affirming its autonomy vis-à-vis all modes of
external expression; in a word, by springing up from the depths
of Arab soil, it gave to the Eastern world its operational framework, its expressive form, and its truth. The genius of Persian
culture had, of course, freed itself from Hellenism under the
Sasanids, but only to be intellectually imprisoned by an inferior

spiritual system. It managed to discover its true self only thanks to Islam. It took the most diverse autochthonous elements of Syria-Mesopotamia to build the Dome of the Rock or the Grand Mosque in Damascus, which drew upon a previously repressed fountain of inspiration released by Islam. More than any other mental activity, even mysticism, art expresses the extraordinary symbiosis between Islam and the Orient, with Islam finding its true home in the Orient, while the Orient acknowledged in Islam its spiritual truth.

But if Islam arrived at a moment when the organism known as "Arab culture" was already practically decrepit, then the splendor of Islam becomes nothing more than the belated classic phase of the Orient. This would readily explain why the Arab empire broke up about the year 800, and why Islamic civilization, which replaced that empire as a unifying and identifying principle, did not open the way to a radical renewal in human life, and in some cases perhaps, merely marked time. The historical enigma of that civilization's rapid decline, while still debatable, can be seen now in a new light. Because, if Spengler is right, Islam would no longer be the dawn of a new world but the twilight of a culture that had found in it the most beautiful and authentic winding sheet possible. And neither Islam nor Arab culture could have any sort of renaissance to look forward to: such is the ultimate and terrifying consequence of Spengler's argument.

The most important thing going on in the recent history of the Orient is that this world is unanimously identifying with the Arab Islamic tradition, when other periods of its rich and varied past might have provided other models for shaping an identity. After all, why not choose Babylon, Phoenicia, pharaonic Egypt, the "oriental" Orient, with all its pomp and splendors? The reason is that Arab-Islam is alive, and that other world is dead. Islam is modern, while the other world is archaic, And, finally, Islam represents a moment of exceptional grandeur, authenticity, and creativity. So Spengler is right to insist on the process of identification, but wrong to limit it temporally, for the realm of his "Magian" humanity is now becoming aware of its Arab-Islamic character and choosing to sacrifice to it all the rest of its history.

As if led by the hidden hand of fate, from the thirteenth century onward the Levant has fallen into a second pseudo-morphosis arising out of the same Greek world and its epigones. A stream of slaves from eastern Europe poured over it and, later, the Ottoman empire almost cost it its soul. In the nine-teenth and twentieth centuries there came the problem of West-ern alienation, however fruitful it may have proved, once it was overcome. When the Levant finally got hold of and discovered itself again, what dimension of its being did this world invoke? The Arab dimension. Once again the Arab way of life is becom-ing the truth and hope of the lost Orient.

Much more, obviously, might be said about the problem of the West. We shall see how the real difficulty raised by Europe's claim to exceptional status must be approached. For Spengler, however, Europe is merely one specific major civilization among others, with a period of supreme achievement lasting two or three hundred years. Iqbal has been quick to criticize Spengler for making too radical a cleavage between Europe and antiquity and for reducing the West to the historical destiny of the former.

Spengler's thought has the great virtue of trying to break out of the rut of its spatio-temporal origins—something Marx failed to do, as he identified Western civilization with civiliza-tion in general, practically consigning the Eastern world to barbarism.[25]

The destiny of the West, in fact, takes its place in a dialectic between universality and particularity. We have seen univer-sality setting in and gathering all contemporary humanity to-gether in a clearly defined historical organism. As a cultural ideal it has manifested itself outside of Europe, which invented it in the first place, and has spread all over the world. As for the particularity to which Spengler reduces the whole existence of the West, it too has gone abroad: the concept of the West has widened and taken on the stature of an absolute, but expanding universality has confined it within the body of the *oikumene*.

The future will no doubt accentuate this phenomenon by particularizing even more the West as against the whole, and Europe as against the West, so that Europe will be above all the specific homeland of a specific people, whose sole contribution will come through their civilization—a circumscribed but nonetheless important contribution for the general civilization of our time.

So Spengler's diagnosis of the decline of the West was accurate, but he did not realize that this decline was much less a failure of creative powers than a loss of a monopoly on universal or world-historical status, the other side of this coin being the concretization of the West as part of global reality. To the extent that Spengler mistakenly lumped together the two levels of the universal and the particular by the simple act of denying the first, he wound up affirming that the decline of the West was the falling off of a particular civilization, whereas what really happened was merely a slippage from one level to another. Spengler was also mistaken, I believe, about the momentum of the West's decline.

The culture-civilization dichotomy is valuable insofar as it calls attention to the slackening of energy within a given society. But why pass off a heroic epoch as a ne plus ultra? Spengler's dating of the cataclysmic break with the past at about 1815 (which buries the nineteenth century under a landslide of contempt) strikes me as a century too early. The eighteenth century, to be sure, remains the age of the most vigorous creations in music, philosophy, science, and politics. Here we have the seedbed of the modern world, the foundation of modern civilization. But by the same token it was a century of stuttering and hesitation on the part of a culture that did not reach completion and master its potential until the nineteenth century—and I mean the nineteenth century in the broad sense, as the era that ended with World War II. Since that time, Western culture, overextended and out of breath, has drastically lowered its sights.

Though it once aimed at universality, Western culture is nonetheless particular. Although it defined modernity,

Western civilization remains specific. And that is why both culture and civilization will have to face the stern law of life: old age and one day, perhaps, death. Except that the whole problem of future history comes down to wondering whether there might not be a new dialectic of the life of civilizations, incommensurable with the dialectic of the past.

# PART II
# ISLAM AND EUROPE:
# TWO HISTORICAL
# STRUCTURES

# 5

# The Historical Dynamic

This essay in comparative history would surely be going off at a tangent were we to turn the parallel between Europe and Islam into a rivalry or, worse yet, a race to achieve industrialization—with Europe winning and the Islamic world badly beaten. Industry is only one aspect of Europe, it represents something like the culmination of originally imperceptible movements. Granted, it is the most universifiable of them all. But about 1830, when Hegel was reflecting on the miracle of Europe and launching into philosophy of history that still commands the greatest interest, was he really aware of the industrial revolution slowly taking place before his eyes?[1]

The superiority of Europe, in his view, was based on the concepts of culture and spirituality, or the emergence of new principles both rational and humane. The whole generation of the *aufklärer* and later that of the pre-Marxian German ideologues, so conscious of the ascent of Europe as the true measure of human progress, was much more attached to intellectual, moral, and cultural achievements than to the starting up of the industrial machine that would eventually devour the world. There was none of the intellectual's aristocratic bias here, but behind this eclipse of the phenomenon of industrialism by the thought of universality there lies the fact that European civilization was already consolidated before the arrival of industrialism. The present-day equation of the two is thus wrong and reductive, and in no way a simple cultural given. Europe's power and imperialism had already set the world ablaze in the sixteenth century—a conflagration that had begun to smolder with the Crusades. There is no historical justification for the feeling that industrialization constitutes a break in the fabric of European life. It was neither a new point of departure nor even a phase of efflorescence.

Industry, which is a quantitative category, was neither the invention of a specific relationship to the world (unlike science) nor the discovery of an original structure of civilization. Rather it subjected the natural world to man on the largest scale ever known. In the nineteenth century its content—what it manufactured—along with its geographic and human framework arose out of previously established structures. If there is any sort of justification nowadays (and only now) in speaking of "industrial civilization," it is because, after more than a century of persevering efforts, this mode of production has penetrated the deepest levels of European society—it has altered people's behavior and way of life, and is beginning to exert a strong influence on the way they think.

But France, Germany, and England are still there; that is, states and nations go on as before, as do national or regional cultural traditions, together with the political systems that have grown out of English parliamentary law and the French Revolution. The quantitative fact of industrialization has been transformed into a qualitative fact of civilization only to a limited extent. And this change has been anything but radical.

Industry cannot be considered the fundamental feature of European existence unless all the other aspects of Europe are to be ground up and absorbed into it. If it is to become the common measure of a new historical era, it will have to spread to the outermost reaches and the inmost depths of the *oikumene*. The process is on the way to completion, but it is far from having come to its evolutionary term. In fact, outside of the European sphere it has just begun.

Since there is more to Europe than industrialism, the recourse to history has yet another meaning: the historical existence of Europe is taking shape as a particular entity. Since industrialism seems likely to provide the basis for the future of the entire human race, any exploration of European history acquires a global dimension. Conversely, if the industrial system is the only product of Europe's genius that is truly exportable, then the other great living civilizations, as integrated, resilient human creations, return once more to the light of universal history—precisely insofar as they have not renounced their historical consciousness.

In what sense is Europe universal? When it conceived of humanity as the ultimate value, when it was put to the test of the facts (e.g., in the days of triumphant imperialism), it engaged in banal, even violent forms of domination, thereby denying its own vision of man. Europe's mercantile and political conquests certainly did spread all over the world, but was that merely the result of the power of its instruments? A fresh look at the epic of Alexander the Great or the exploits of the Arab conquest will make it clear that there was no less audacity displayed there, no less endurance and rude energy, than in European efforts to subjugate the world. Finally, with its grand universalist ideal, did Europe link together all human cultures? It can safely be said that never before did such intense curiosity reach out to explore so many different horizons.

But it must also be said that no imperial civilization was ever less consciously receptive to outside influences: neither the popularity of Chinese art or African sculpture nor the influence of Japanese prints on Impressionism can offer sufficient evidence to argue for any real syncretism under the banner of the European mind. Medieval and Renaissance Europe unquestionably borrowed more than modern Europe from the outside world—Islam, China, or antiquity—even though in earlier times there was less direct and familiar contact with it. After it had won more self-assurance and consolidated its gains, Europe showed itself less amenable to foreign influence.

Europe's first attitude was one of humility, and this played a large part in its rapid advance. So the externalist hypothesis can be applied only to this early stage, when Europe was in its infancy, not to the later stage when it laid claim to universality. And this hypothesis should under no circumstances be confused with the idea of Europe as the inheritor of all past civilizations, as if those civilizations had bequeathed everything they could to Europe and to it alone.

If we turn now to the parts of itself that a triumphant Europe exported, we are struck by their omnipresence. Does not every city outside Europe have its European double? Every country has its own language, plus one or more European languages. Every nation, even at the heart of its historical continuity, bears an ancient past plus a specifically colonial past. Africa is at least as much unified by its African identity as it is partitioned by its French- and English-speaking regions. Even the individual self breaks down into an autochthonous base and a European patina.

Europe thus penetrated the world at the very moment when its overseas empire was in retreat. And if tomorrow by some misfortune the continent itself should crumble into nothingness, another Europe might well arise from the ruins, to live on in the minds and hearts of the people it had once so stubbornly denied. What is universal about Europe is the seeds that it sowed here and there, as if by accident. The universal element is also the least European aspect of Europe's creative achievements: science, critical thought, certain kinds of philosophical questioning, and ethical choices. Hence, if the material culture of Europe has impregnated so much of the world, it is due not to its particularity but to its rationality. But the most disconcerting thing here is surely the fact that some of the least European of Europe's creations, such as science, derive in some fashion from the European ethos.

High European culture certainly aimed at universality, but this was more an ideal than a reality. That culture was doomed by a painful fate to be imprisoned in its local historical roots, and it proved in addition to be the target of periodic resurgence by the most particularist forces, such as nationalism. Reason in itself has by definition a universalizing tendency, but its successive manifestations have flowered in a soil of barbarism and, later, of organized violence. Cartesian rationality had to grow amid fear and repressive silence, the critical reason of the Enlightenment faced an outdated political system, and dialectical reason a savagely unjust social order.

In other words, Europe's intellectual conquests will always be overcast by the problem of the antinomy between the particular and the universal. Their obviously European character is no justification for denying the universal import of the rational categories that have sprung up so abundantly in Europe, but neither can the constant presence of that character be ignored. This explains why it is so hard to transplant a kind of rationality so intimately bound up with a historical tradition. Which raises the issue of the relations between history and reason, history and value, history and universality.

In what way and to what degree can a civilization be outstripped by its own achievements? But, also, to what degree are these achievements imprisoned by the civilization that produced them? Without going so far as to say that Europe's accomplishments will not truly live until Europe dies, it can be argued that Europe will no longer be able to live by taking refuge behind those accomplishments. If it is assumed that other civilizations will obstinately survive, there is no reason why Europe should not do the same. But once Europe is separated from its historic achievements, it will be no more than a partner in the larger task that occupies all of humanity, which will no longer be defined by Europe, but in terms of its own conflicting diversity, by a concrete universality based on a truly common experience.

## EUROPE AGAINST EUROPE

Despite the historical connection that I have described, the part of Europe which will survive as a possible foundation for some sort of universality comprises things that concrete, empirical history repressed, denied, or obscured. Marxism, for example, failed in its original homeland, but it caused profound upheavals outside Europe, in the Soviet Union and China, which led to an intellectual resurgence in Europe. But what, we may ask, did Marxism represent in the history of nineteenth-century Europe? It represented one critical current, among others, in a nascent industrial society. And the birth and development of that society are the key to the nineteenth century.

At the very moment when the bourgeoisie was setting itself up, on all levels, as embodying the central theme of European history and the driving force behind it, Marx exalted the counterforce of the proletariat, conferring on it a mission that the bourgeoisie was in the process of carrying out. Marx's vision became a hope paradoxically fulfilled. There is no surprise in the fact that this vision should find a home in places where no solid bourgeoisie existed. Like Jesus, Marx preached to his people that the kingdom of heaven was at hand. Like Christianity, Marxism was rejected, only to prosper far from the land of its birth. Germany would make its way into the charmed circle of universality not through its militaristic spirit nor through its industrial might nor even through an imperialism wholly oriented toward the European arena, but through its philo-sophical vigor and the critical methodology of its scholars, which were passed on to the entire world through French intermediaries.

And yet how many of Germany's creative geniuses were honored in their own country? One recalls Hölderlin's despair, the *Zerrissenheit* of the whole Romantic generation, Nietzsche's descent into madness and death. For all that, the philistines were as numerous as ever. But Nietzsche found thoughtful readers as far away as Iqbal in Lahore, while Hegel and Marx provoked the intelligentsia all over the world into writing commentaries.

Living cultures, of course, characteristically look toward posterity. They are not always denied by real history, but the latter operates in its own present and has its own tasks to accomplish. Nevertheless, in the case of Europe, which offers itself to the outside world as the homeland of Galileo, Descartes,

Voltaire, and Hegel, we see a derisory contrast between its claims and the lowly place it has so often assigned to the great creative spirits who spoke for it to others. There is, in other words, a vast distance separating the empirical, even the historical Europe from the creative Europe, source of the idea of universality.

From this point of view, the two or three hundred men who worked out the conceptual grid of scientific and philosophical thought, who defined the values or the aesthetic principles of the modern world, are not an illustration of European history. Rather it is European history that becomes the framework and support of their activity. If industrialized Europe can be considered a model, then the Europe of foundational thinking, of intelligence, reason, and the new aesthetics—at the two high points of the Renaissance and the eighteenth century—must be considered the originator of universality in the modern sense as well as a moment of universal history. Because Europe could not be a model for all non-Europeans, except to the very unlikely extent that it should aspire to provide the world of the future with another, radically different approach. Should this happen, Europe would be rejected just when its creative spirit was being imitated.

## Islam as a Universalizing, Historicizing, and Mediating Agent

A period of creative enthusiasm does not necessarily have any de facto universal significance. If modern Europe can boast of such significance, it is because it has conquered the world; and it conquered because it was ready and because the structure of modern history enabled it to do so. If its dynamic energy had been directed along lines other than those of omnicompetent rationality, would it have reached its goals in the world? And it was crucial that that explosion of European energy should have occurred at the specific moment it did. The first point relates to both the internal and the external scene (influences, salvaging of the past), whereas the second relates exclusively to the domain of universal history. Insofar as it is a civilization firmly set on its own foundation, evolving in accordance with its own inner logic, attached to a certain number of concrete forms, Europe can be compared historically and anthropologically with the civilization of Islam. One might draw a parallel between these two cultural dynamisms, these two kinds of totalization, by neglecting their concrete duration or rather by replacing them with transchronic correspondences à la Spengler. I shall return to this point later on but for the moment let us concentrate on universal history. Universal history cannot be properly defined as a collection of determinate historical organisms, each evolving in its own sphere, nor in a theatrical perspective where the actors of history, one after another, hold the center of the stage, nor still less as a simple political claim to world empire. It is clear that universality is bound up with the present-day process, which is moving us toward one world, just as it is obvious that if we are headed in this direction, it was never reached in the past.

Earlier universal history would then be viewed as all of a piece, as the long underground tunnel whence modernity will one day issue. But all of history cannot be put on one of the balance scales of time and European history, beginning with the great discoveries, on the other. There was, rather, the first preuniversal and Neolithic civilization (the Orient, Greece, Rome), followed by the second stage of history, post-Neolithic and universalizing, which founded the modern world we live in. This history, to be sure, was not fully integrated on all levels, since each of its components (Europe, Islam, Byzantium, China, India) thought of itself as a finished, autotelic world. But these differences, far from running counter to the factors promoting convergence, proved to be a primordial condition for the progress of civilization. Thus the emergence of Europe cannot be thought of apart from that totality. And, in any event, what does Europe's special status mean? It cannot be gauged by a content that one might relativize at any time, but in a global context such that at a certain point Europe came to surpass and dominate its partners.

Modern Europe was the last moment, and perhaps for that reason the most crucial moment, of an extremely fertile era in the history of humanity, an era inaugurated by the birth and expansion of Islam. Why Islam? Because analysis shows it to be the axis around which the world system would turn. Neither the fall of the Roman Empire in the West and the establishment in its wake of the barbarian kingdoms, nor the foundation of the unified Chinese Empire in the third century B.C., nor the slow and confused emergence of India constitute a solid, clear, and consistent point of departure.

It was Islam—and not, evidently, their own particular cultural roots—that the other groups used to define themselves as parts of a system. And it was then that the *oikumene* expanded, that technological conquests forged ahead, that the nations of the future awoke to a sense of their destiny. We are all, in the deepest fibers of our being, the children of that age at the end of which came the dawn of a universal evolutionary process.

This creates a powerful obligation not to assign any special value to any one civilization, no more to Islam than to Europe or to China. If the final period (and within that the final subperiod, i.e., the industrial era) enjoys a certain privileged status, that is because a direct hereditary connection links it to modernity. There remains the intimate and profound domain of historical existence that by a reverse movement links up with the inaugural period—which is what makes the Muslim a Muslim, the Chinese a Chinese, the European a European.

Only a vision of history fixated on the West could have compared the Middle Ages to a gigantic parenthesis between antiquity and the modern age, calling it a time of darkness, a vast lacuna. In this view "the West," a notion subsuming that of Europe, refers to a historical tradition going all the way back to the Greeks, passing through Rome and, after lying hidden during the Middle Ages, resurfacing in the Renaissance. This highly ideological reading of the past played a crucial role as an energizing illusion in Europe's aesthetic and intellectual renewal. Today it is simply a nostalgic relic and the last bastion of a sense of privilege bestowed by the magical hand of history.

What it says, in effect, is that only one basic approach, that of the humanistic civilizations, has proved fertile. Everything else has just led to an impasse. What are China, Islam, India?— impressive cultural flowerings with no future and nothing to say to the modern world.

Things were different in the past, when the awareness of a deeply human cultural tradition did nothing, essentially, except express a new passion for civilization, progress, and development, a passion that sprang up in the immediately preceding epoch.

The fact that medieval Europe—a weak link or long period of latency—played only a modest role in the shaping of the future world is no reason why this age of preparation should be belittled or ignored. While barbarism was casting its shadow over a fragile and unformed Europe in the seventh century, the Arabs were embarked on a triumphant campaign. On the one hand, the void of the tenth century A.D., on the other, the fullness of the fourth century after the Hijra, the high point of Islamic classicism. In one instance we have regression (a notion of the Middle Ages skewed by its preoccupation with antiquity), in the other—and this occurs not on the fringes of the world but at its center—expansion, organization, upward movement.

There is never any regression in history as a whole, only in certain specific historical organisms. The great concentrations of cultural energy migrate from place to place and raise earlier human achievements to a higher level. The Great Regression that Malraux talks about, stretching from Gallia Narbonensis to Transoxiana, was no doubt the end of a given world, but it was still more a gestation period, which culminated in the formation of the living tissue of the next two thousand years. A new East—Islam and China—gave the first impulse to a gigantic thrust of creativity, organization, and civilization.[2] It was a fertile period, like all the others, and not a "middle age"; it was a spreading of human spaces and a deepening of the range of intuition, a broad advance by peoples sprung from nowhere, and an age of crucial technological conquests. Above all, despite some ideological conflicts, the compartments separating civilizations were broken down: now there were only communities engaged in a common adventure, in unconscious solidarity. Modern Europe was the offspring of this age, and Islam was its progenitor.

Medieval Christendom was not so much a particularized structure comparable to Byzantium, or a reminiscence of the Empire, as a mobilizing response of Europe to Islam, an expressive pattern that climaxed in the Crusades, which were a counterattack, a stepping outside the self, an outpouring of energy, a school of civilization for Europe. The Iberian Peninsula, which led the way in the subjection of the world to Europe, found its identity during the long adventure of the *Reconquista* only because of its duel with Islam. Historians ordinarily stress technological and cultural borrowings. A far more important factor here, it seems to me, is the political dialectic between the self and the world through which Europe perceived itself as a coherent unit—which once again raises the problem of the actual genesis of Europe. From this point of view the theses proposed by Pirenne and Lombard are not contradictory but complementary. Islam was at once a military force threatening Europe and an economic sphere sharing its dynamism, just as later it would be an ideological enemy and a philosophical model. In a word, Europe's emergence into history took place— and could not have taken place otherwise—through the mediation of Islam: in the beginning by means of a defensive recoil, afterward by an offensive explosion.

Furthermore, almost everywhere, the peoples of the known world awoke to self-awareness or made their entrance into history through some sort of contact with Islam. Even the Chinese, as autonomous as they were, owed a debt to Islam for introducing them into the global circuit of exchange.[3] India was profoundly shaken by the victories of Qutayba b. Muslim and later by those of Mahmud of Ghazna. As for the black African world, which was absolutely unknown and isolated in antiquity, its partial and still hesitating entrance into the historical arena was likewise due to Islam. And then there were the Russians (*Rus* in Arabic), the Volga Bulgarians, the Turkomans: so many barbarian peoples had their apprenticeship in civilization by passing through Islam. In the process they undoubtedly weakened Islam's cohesiveness as a political power, but they also made Islamic civilization their common creative achievement.

If Europe, that promontory of Asia, survived and asserted itself, it was because it had the advantage of a thousand years of peace, from the end of the Magyar invasions to that other "thirty years war," 1914–1945.[4] And it devolved upon Islam to be the protective screen between Europe and the great waves of violence; it was Islam that absorbed the deadly poison of the Mongol hordes; Islam that later stopped Tamerlane, whose armies were at least as destructive as the Mongols, if not more. The havoc they wreaked was not justified by the fact that they converted to Islam, any more than Islam was glorified by the mausoleums of Samarkand built over the ruins of the old city center.

## REREADING WORLD HISTORY

The destruction of the cultural core of Syrian-Iraqi Islam implied neither a loss of power nor a contraction of civilizing influence. Because new forces were arising on its periphery, in particular the future Ottoman and Mogul empires, which annexed two hitherto autonomous areas to the domain of Islam, Byzantium fell; India and then Indonesia were swept up into the Islamic sphere of influence. The multipolarity of the world was narrowed to three principal axes: the Islamic (now split into many cultural subtraditions), the Western, and the Chinese. Historians have argued that the year 1300 represents the point at which Islam got the upper hand over its rivals—this is not, obviously, the Islam of the first Abbasids, not a monolithic empire but a civilization in the making, an Islam that stretched out simultaneously toward the Far East and toward Europe. This was an Islam with a finished, mature, fully coherent civilization, displaying a coherent identity over a vast geographical range. And it is perfectly true that in 1600, after a century of the European Renaissance (which can also be legitimately viewed as a small local flowering), the greater part of the human race found itself in Islamic territory.[5] The *oikumene* seemed to be hedged about on all sides by Islam, which occupied a central position because it was the only one of its worldwide partners in constant contact with all

the others. The Occident was warped in upon itself, forced into
a peninsular posture, moving about within a reduced space; it
could not communicate with the outside world, except through
Islam or Byzantium. Similarly, China, which controlled the
larger part of the Far East, as a civilizing nucleus surrounded
by its satellites, had outside ties only with India and Islam.

This point of view rejects the familiar West-centered approach, restores the thickness and actuality to real historical
time and, finally, revises the Arab-centered vision of Islam,
which is fixated on the epoch of the great Arabian caliphate,
but it raises many questions. Which Islam, after all, are we
talking about? The Ottomans were Muslims, but many other
things as well, and the same holds for the Moguls of India and
the Safavids. By this time the Arabs has vanished from the
scene. Islam remained, of course, but as a coherent religion,
not as a live, creative, unifying culture, except perhaps on the
level of art. And at the very moment when Islam was expanding spatially, not only was it losing much of its cultural resili-
ency but it saw its vital roots, especially in commerce, being
gnawed away by Europeans.

This led to a second decline for its central regions, which
had enjoyed the privilege of forging a successful synthesis of
religion, culture, and politics. We must, therefore, be wary of
the way Arabs and Muslims in general, but Europeans too,
have glorified the classicism of the caliphate. Equally dubious
is the new emphasis on the later history of Islam, locating its
apogee five centuries later, based on the triple evidence of
(short-lived) military supremacy, the spread of religious faith,
and the stabilization of tradition. Sinan in Turkey, Akbar's
architects and painters in India, the Safavid mystics in Iran, all
had fine, grand, sublime achievements to their credit. But was
this an integrated culture? How did it relate to the Islamic
legacy? Was there a renewed vision of the world, an intellectual self-awareness? The fact remains that a large portion of
humanity, nation after nation, was swept into the ranks of
Islam and, over ten centuries, these peoples played a central,
dominant, pace-setting role, driven by Islam's will to power.
As late as 1500, Islam's great rival was not Western Europe,

but China—a rival on the objective level of cultural achievements rather than a keenly felt competitive one. Byzantium and India proved to be weak points. And finally the West, small as it was, prevailed over the rest of the world, whereas about 1200, civilization in Western Europe still seemed behind the times.

This burst of expansion will always strike us, its contemporary witnesses, as an enigma. Because we experience it from one side or the other, we view it as an anomaly or a triumph, in the excess of historical consciousness that characterizes our day. In fact, Europe's upward surge was based mainly on its jealously guarded autonomy and, secondarily, on a movement out of itself, in time and space. At the moment when the greater part of humanity lived in the shadow of Islam, after the destruction of Byzantium and the annexation of India, only two regions maintained their independence: China and the West. The autonomy, the insularity, the particularism of each of these regions make their destinies altogether comparable, except that, before the discovery of America, Europe was more physically confined within itself, while Chinese tradition held sway over a wider area, from Japan to Annam. It was precisely its defensive posture, its remoteness, its marginality, and the narrow limits of its territory that drove the West to do so much all by itself, to rely on its own potential, but also to show a certain humility toward its "closest mentors,"[6] Byzantium and Islam, and to venture out toward wider geographical and historical horizons: America on the one hand, ancient Greece on the other. In this, Europe was different from China. As isolated as China, as jealous of its independence, the West developed through internal mobilization of its resources—which led to successive revolutions. And it showed greater openness than China to the outside world, or perhaps it was thrust outward by its heterogeneous makeup, its weak capacity as a civilizing agent, its barbaric vitality and, at bottom, mixed in with its feverish pride, by a certain humility. The West had cultivated an inferiority complex toward Islam, whereas in the Far East China maintained a haughty silence on the subject.

The paradox of the West is that all its creations have drawn on its own resources and yet, at the same time, these creations have revealed an irresistible need for externalization, whence the violence wreaked on the outside world, the use of foreign models, the recurrent messianism. This is what brought about the clearing of the northern forests and the Crusades, the Renaissance and colonial settlements in America, industrialization and imperialism. But this connection is not a necessary one: what is shown here may be a dialectical pattern or no pattern at all. Before the nineteenth century, did Europe deliberately seek world hegemony? Even after 1900 Europe remained fundamentally preoccupied with itself, which led to its self-destruction as a center of political power, to fragmentation, to the reemergence of other societies that had been reshaped by the momentary intrusion of the West and that were the bearers of entirely fresh points of view.

# 6

# Islam: Civilization, Culture, Politics

At the time barbarian Europe was passing through its incubation period and lay in a state of fragile vulnerability, a unique historical presence was coming to light—Islam, a presence that would occupy the center of the world stage for almost a thousand years, first as an empire, then as a civilization. This Islam is first apparent as an agent in the general flow of history but, beyond that, it also had its specific features—a color, a temporal rhythm, and a fundamental inspiration all its own.

So there are two Islams to be investigated: one is part of an integral world history, while the other evolves in empirical history as a complex totality, at once a religion, a civilization, and a political and cultural organism. Unlike Islam in its universal aspect, this Islam is focused on its own interior life and thinks of itself as a self-contained world. We shall take the same approach toward Europe, except that Europe's specific character seems to lie in continuous movement rather than in any synthetic totality.

## ISLAMIC CIVILIZATION

From the temporal standpoint, this civilization emerged as Islam's political empire effectively disintegrated (third to ninth century after the Hijra). The first Islamic century was one of conquest and domination, the second, one of adjusting that fact to the ideological-religious facts as well as to the aspirations of the subjected peoples. But the Abbasid caliphate at its height gave way to a multitude of political and cultural centers which, in the following centuries, definitively established and spread widely a civilization that had hitherto been localized and hesitant, and which ultimately took three centuries to reach formal perfection. Just when the tide of Arab expansion was turning, a civilization largely inspired by the Arabs was settling in, all the way to the borders of central Asia. Just when a state professing the Islamic religion saw its power slipping, that same faith was making converts among the Iranian aristocracy, the Aramaeans of the Mesopotamian Sawad, the Copts and, in the far west, the Iberians. It was then that the various pre-Islamic cultural traditions welled up from the depths of a past hitherto denied, and Islamic civilization reached its most advanced degree of unity. This civilization was a coherent whole but diversely accented by the genius of the peoples belonging to it, a civilization born out of its subjugation but still more out of its subsequent freedom. Without that freedom, which was seized as much as it was granted, Islamic civilization would doubtlessly not have enjoyed such formidable growth in time and space. Would it have taken hold at all? Because the moment came when a great wind of uncertainty blew across the old Orient—now renewed and liberated—over in what direction its present and future culture should go. And both Islam and the Arab way of life were called into question. Then in the eleventh century a choice was made in their favor, echoing the choice made two centuries before by the jurists who opted for the Islamization of society. The sudden awareness of Islamic spirituality that occurred in Kufa, Basra, and Medina circa 722 was not a forgone conclusion, any more than the triumph of Arabian Islam over Hellenism and Iranian culture was in 922. But Islam found a permanent home in the East, just as the East found a source of energy in Islam. After that, Arab-Islamic civilization could spread beyond its earliest focal points.

Unified and diverse, Arab-Islamic at its core, but shot through with a thousand contrasting influences, multiform, evolutionary yet faithful to the spirit of its founding Revelation, synthetic but powerfully original, this civilization, which shone with intense brilliance for five centuries, represents one of the most sublime efforts in human history. "Never," Hegel wrote of Islam, "has sheer enthusiasm accomplished greater deeds." A civilization, to be sure, is judged by the creative vigor with which it gives a particular shape to the adventure of life, as well as by its values. And yet those values, which always escape us because we see them from the outside, are things that people drew sustenance from and appropriated with joy, after tirelessly working them out and diffusing them. But does not Islam's greatest glory lie in the union it forged among people?

Islam's material civilization was the powerful base on which the whole cultural edifice loosely rested: a "hydraulic" civilization, but a commercial, urban one as well. Attaching itself to the fringes of the desert, it stretched all along the great rivers, the Euphrates, the Tigris, the Nile, the Oxus, the Jaxartes, the seedbeds of the most ancient cultures. It thus shows its true colors—as a remarkable conquest over an environment at once hostile, fragile, and brilliant. This agricultural system presupposes careful organization, intervention on the part of the state, and a bureaucracy, but it serves as a congenial environment for despotism and oppression.

From the *huertas* (irrigated lands) of Andalusia to the oases of the Maghrib, to the valley of the Nile, the Sawad of Iraq, and all the way to Farghana, the people who carried the Islamic world and its life on their backs were the peasants and the forgotten, downtrodden slaves of the land. And should a historical accident occur—an invasion, a revolt, a weakening of the state structure—and the steppe regain the upper hand, public works would be abandoned, and the specter of regression would appear.

Islamic civilization was eminently urban and commercial. The Arab conquest had prompted an intense urbanization, both in the regions destined to become permanently Arab as well as

in Iran. This process was the result of a master plan, a conscious
intention, but it developed along with the overall growth of the
Muslim world, incorporating as it went along whole waves of
immigrants from the countryside.

In the beginning, the camp-cities of Kufa, Basra, and Fustat
were projections of the Arab way of life onto a non-Arab world
that had been subjugated by force. They were the shared home
of whole or fragmentary tribal groups that had been torn from
the endless expanse of the Arabian steppes and were now
constrained to live together tamely after having known the
hard, irresponsible freedom of the desert.

Yet this changeover to a sedentary life went off without a
hitch, with positively baffling ease. The camp-city, quickly
demilitarized, was transformed into a civilian city, with its
principal mosque, its built-up *suqs*, its meeting places, aristocratic houses, and neighborhood mosques, its *hammams*, its
tribal plots of land changed into urban districts, its burgeoning
suburbs. Kufa, which had been so markedly Arab in the seventh
century, so full of the dust and odors of the desert, inhabited
by Yemenite aristocrats, of Rabi'a and Mudar, gave way to a
*medina* that was banal but complex, with permanent buildings, a
rendezvous for a variety of distinct functional worlds: plebe-
ians, patricians, trade guilds, *'ulama*, officers. The Islamic city
emerged from the shadows to present itself, from then on, as
the ideal framework for Muslim life, the home of Muslim civilization, the core of an intensely social existence strongly influenced by culture and religion.

With his nervous, alert style Massignon manages to capture
the palpitating life of the Islamic city, its richness and its fatal
contradictions, in the age when its features hardened under the
imprint of classicism:

> Basra was not simply a city of refuge, a place for shelter-
> ing, in jumbled fashion, women, children, slaves, and
> booty from raids . . . it quickly became a complete me-
> tropolis, an important agricultural center, an innovator of
> industrial techniques, a high-rise platform, not for a

Greek-style parliamentary theatre putting on plays and
trials, but for pedagogical communication, for a Semitic
university, transmitting intellectual patterns. . . . The
growth of Basra was a brief but lively crisis in the growth of
Arab culture, as it has been studied by ibn Khaldun.

Owing to the political instability that from the eleventh
century on proved to be a constant in the history of Islam, the
Islamic city experienced a permanent social dialectic. There was
a proliferation of sects, and schools of law flourished, but there
was also unrest, class conflict, disorder among the youth. The
cultural and social crises turned into chronic conditions, but no
changes were made in the social structure, in political gov-
ernance or ideological inspiration. This sort of maturity in a
civilization that grew old too quickly sheds a melancholy cre-
puscular light on the fury of history, when the noblest revolutionary intentions run headlong up against its inertia, get
bogged down, and die.

This model of a unified civilization, with the city as its
privileged framework, took shape during the tenth and eleventh centuries, mobilizing its entire potential in an immense
process that would develop and perfect itself over the next two
centuries. Bound to a religion and a certain way of life, this
civilization not only imposed its norms on a varied assortment
of politically divided societies but wished to be the norm for all
generations to come: it thought it had reached perfection. But
this belief was undoubtedly based less on this civilization's
brilliance than on its internal coherence. For although its own
children leveled violent charges against this or that aspect of it,
they never attacked its whole being. Its survival was guaranteed
by the fact that the generations who lived within its pale came to
love it and make it their own.

In Herat, Merv, Rayy, Damascus, Aleppo, Baghdad, Cairo,
Kairouan, and Córdoba the situation was the same, with variations, and it affected every kind of activity, from the highest to
the lowest. About 1150, however, another age began, post-
Seljuk in the East, post-Hilal in the Maghrib; and the aggressive

rise of the West began to exert more pressure. The nomadic invasions profoundly altered a fragile equilibrium, eventually to be shattered by the advance of the Mongol hordes. If Islam survived, it was precisely because of its call to civilization and, still more, because of the universality of its genuinely spiritual message. But Islamic civilization came out of the crisis with its powers diminished, its nature reshaped—a different kind of thing.

## ISLAMIC CULTURE

The high culture of classical Arab Islam was not fully represented, as critics have always maintained, by its legal dimension, nor by the rationalism of *falsafa* or the tendency to mysticism, as an increasingly popular approach would have it. The concept of Arab Islam does not deal with a portion of a more comprehensive culture, any more than it is exhausted by the career of a man like ibn Qutayba. It encompasses all the branches of the tree of Islamic culture; it is fundamentally unified both in its theoretical bearings and in its practical behavior. During a productive period five centuries long one common cultural language and the omnipresent horizon of Revelation spanned geographical and mental space, linking Khurasan and Spain, Avicenna and Averroes, but also Averroes the jurist and Averroes the materialist philosopher. The unity of a culture also involves the feeling of oneness, the desire to be one. It would therefore be pointless for Orientalism, whether out of malice or ignorance, to try to reduce Arab Islam to its philological and legal elements, to narrow it down before devaluing it.

Intellectual enthusiasm directed all the steps taken by the Islamic mind, but so did a passion for autonomy. This culture pursued all the forms of learning with fierce vigor: history, geography, law, scholastic theology, philosophy, medicine, mathematics. But in the meantime it was seized and shaken by an underlying force: a fascination with God. It was, after all, a culture focused on God. And this religious quest still haunts us. For although European science has penetrated into the most forbidding depths of the physical world, the question still remains whether the world is worthy of the mind's efforts to grasp it. Nietzsche said some time ago that the only purpose of science is to arm us for action. But the essence of the mind is to transport us beyond worldly appearances to that which is absolute value and mind itself. Now, for Muslims, God had spoken; then silence came down upon a world deprived of God. And so it was necessary to study the text, which was more beautiful and sublime than the world because it embodied the traces of God's fleeting appearance.

Of all the high cultures based on religion, Islamic culture had the strongest sense of God, "making the knowledge of that One alone the unique goal of reality," as Hegel correctly understood. However profound its Christian inspiration, as recorded in its cathedrals and iconography, Europe did not really succeed in exploring God; and after the great schism of the Reformation it committed itself to the world while taking man to be the supreme value.

Here and there, however, great thinkers came up against a formidable barrier: the abstraction called God and the other abstraction called man, which was a live, vibrant passion. To be sure, Europe offered the world its pietàs and its visions of Christ laid in his tomb, but this was the pain of humanity grasped through God, whereas all of Islam felt a tremendous obsession with the invisible God. Men of different cultures and races were convinced that, not long before, an immense event had taken place, that there had been a moment of power in the history of the world, a moment so close that it was almost within their grasp.

And this conviction spread down through the centuries, as Islam became a religion of the masses, a conviction (shared from the outset with some non-Arabs) that was a thirst for something better than life, something that transcended the misery of life: for God, who is perhaps both within and without us. The mystics believed that Revelation had revealed them to themselves, it had plunged them into the adventure of investigating the self, because in Islam the self and God are continually encountering each other. The men of learning, the '*ulama*, were more aware of the historicity of Revelation, of its singular, that is to say, exceptional, status. This was the origin of the science of religion: of *hadith* and *tafsir*, religious history and theology—the instinctive desire for knowledge at work in a privileged area, not devotion but the unveiling of truth and the continuation, by means of humble, modest knowledge, of the Prophet's grand adventure. This too was the origin of the view of the sacred not as terror or anxiety but as the sphere within which we project the most serious part of ourselves. The science of God is ontology, the science of the Prophet is history or law, but God is holier than those things, and the Prophet, too, became increasingly revered.

## POLITICS IN ISLAM

Religion, civilization, culture: these are powerful parts of the whole of Islam. But what about politics? Nineteenth-century Orientalists sensitized Western opinion to the idea of political religion, to a structure in which religion and politics combine to make Islam an aggressive, hostile, explosive force. Fear of Islam's power to mobilize when in tragic times it accentuates defense, struggle, and conflict (one of the most intensely emotional accents in history), has given rise to the notion of political Islam as a recurrent menace. It has likewise posed the concept of political religion as a basic historical structure of early Islam. Islam, says Goldziher, secularized religion.[1] It aimed at founding a kingdom of this world with the means of this world. And for Snouck-Hurgronje, who was more closely connected with colonial operations, Islam "entered the world as a political religion and owes its universal significance to that alliance of two theoretically incompatible principles."[2] We should understand this to mean an exceptionally successful synthesis: Islam is a real religion, with creed, code, and cult; and the caliphate was a real state and later a real empire. But exceptional arrangements cannot become permanent structures, which is why Islam survived as a religion and the Empire rapidly collapsed, why Islam expanded across the ruins of the Empire.

This is exactly where the link should be broken: Islam did not become universal until after the particularity of its political dimension was obliterated. But because the primitive period managed to bind together the passionate need for God and the self-affirmation of a community, a predisposition, a language, an accent harking back to this fusion has remained. It was not an appeal from politics to religion used in a positive way to organize a state or society, but a polemical pathos whose attractiveness rested on the supportive emotional values of brotherhood, community, and union. The strength of Islam lies in its proven ability to express the poetry of collective life: not the frenzy stirred by modern-style demagogues, but the dramatic intensity of earnest moments. It is also powerful because there is more to it than that.

The political element in Islam is neither a conception of power nor that power itself, nor the search for a principle to organize society as a political body, but pure nostalgia for the primitive era together with a need for defensive military might. The Umayyad Empire was at once a tribal Arabian state and an Oriental monarchy; the Abbasid state was a renovated Sasanid monarchy with an attenuated form of despotism; the hereditary states were local monarchies pure and simple, their energy deriving precisely from the monarchical principle itself. The illusion that politics predominates in the religious existence of Islam has foisted itself on certain thinkers because the upsurge of religious feeling, lacking an institutional framework similar to the Church in western Christianity, often poured out, during Islam's first five centuries, into a tireless search for the ideal government.

The Abbasid Caliphate, in fact, simply oscillated between prevailing ideological trends, whether elitist *mu'tazilism* or populist traditionalism, to cite only two. It did not fashion an ideology of the State any more than its predecessor succeeded in dissolving the Arab tribal structure into a new political entity. Though powerless to mold society, to mark off the boundaries of civilization and culture, the classical Islamic state was nonetheless a strong factor in other domains. Though it was not creative with regard to ideological forces or major cultural choices, early on it displayed considerable alertness and vigilance. It was never indifferent to the pulsations of ideas the way an underpoliticized state might have been. It permitted, encouraged—or, on the contrary, restrained—certain movements, neither leading the way nor remaining truly disinterested. In the socioeconomic realm it acted both as a power that had inherited earlier structures and as an imperial state born of conquest, but not as a purely Islamic state. This led to its seizure of a large part of the economy and the social organism and marked it as a rather strong state, though much weaker than the pressurized state, whether on the ancient (Pharaonic Egypt) or contemporary (China) model.

The Islamic state was unquestionably oppressive, but when it was missing from the scene or its presence was reduced, all sorts of catastrophes resulted, as evidenced by a lowering of the vigor of civilization, the redoubtable effects of the Turco-Mongol invasions, the collapse of Iraq between the thirteenth and nineteenth centuries, the basic cultural weakness of the central Maghrib. Yet we should add that although political authority succeeded in dominating the economic sphere, it failed to do the same in the ideological or cultural. This crucial distinction must be made in order to appreciate the respective roles of the state and of society. In China the state came first, then came civilization, and then religions, in the plural. With Islam, religion, in the singular, came first, then a civilization and culture, both deriving as much from religion as from the accident of conquest and its corollary, the Empire. If the Chinese state was never challenged, it was because it did not grow as a result of being conquered, hence the political cohesiveness of present-day China. But China did not discover its universal mission until quite recently. And so we have another paradox: China today is being culturally shattered, as it denies its essence and its past.

For its part, Islam had long been familiar with a universal goal, but it could never concretize it in a durable, integrated political organism, perhaps because there were two antipodal forces at work here. One may regret that the Ottoman empire, the best organized state in Islam and the one closest to the Western world, got so bogged down in conquering Christian territory, which it did not even try to assimilate, instead of concentrating on the organization and integration of genuinely Islamic regions. This means that Jamal Eddine's intuition was profoundly true: a vast political structure already in existence, a gift of history, endowed with a strong principle of unity (Islam) was a great opportunity absurdly wasted. But the harm was already done. In various ways and at various stages of its history the Ottoman Empire fell prey to the temptation of Europe; that is, the push toward the West and the nineteenth-century movement of Europeanization that gave rise to the Young Turks and, finally, to Atatürk.

## CONTINUITY AND DISCONTINUITY

In the past, Islam has always been guided by the leadership of a particular people or culture, a leadership at first purely Arab, then Iranian-Arab, and later Turco-Iranian. Eventually it was dismembered into a number of cultural units which were projected into territorial space where they settled and solidified. This idea might prove quite useful, if we sharpened its focus, because it sheds light on the problem of continuity and discontinuity better than the rather hollow dyads of apogee/ decline, decadence/renaissance, Arab/non-Arab, orthodoxy/ heterodoxy, not to mention the recent dialectic between tradition and modernity.

The first Islam, then, was a compact whole, historically controlled by one people, whether or not it was endowed with a strong national culture. The second Islam was characterized by multipolarity, thereby ceasing to be an integrated historical agent. This is the fundamental split in Islam. Under the Arabs of the Umayyad epoch all of Islam formed a concentrated unit; similarly the Iraqi-Iranian core of the great Abbasid caliphate held all of Islam within its grasp, and the Seljuk sultanate tried to do the same thing, as did the Fatimid caliphate.

Nowadays, however, we can speak only of hyphenated domains: Arab-Islamic, Iranian-Islamic, Turkish-Islamic, Afro-Islamic, Indo-Islamic, all of them concretized on the map and rooted in a specific cultural tradition. This breakup transformed Islam, not because it divided it politically but because it destroyed a living network of human and cultural exchanges, condemning each region to a solitary existence or to an exclusive dialogue with the past. Perhaps we should date the beginning of this era of partition from the death of Tamerlane, and locate its culmination in the twentieth century, after World War I, between the collapse of the Ottoman caliphate and the emergence of newly independent states from colonialism. In the Muslim world the period from the fifteenth to the eighteenth and even the nineteenth century was an obscure, though vitally important one. It was marked by a slowdown of communications on every level and the dissolution of bonds linking Islamic communities. To what extent, for example, were the Muradites aware of the architectural achievements of the Moguls in India, or even of their existence? In the seventeenth century did the Safavids know what was going on in Algeria, did the scholars of Fez know about the books being written in Lahore or Qom or al-Najaf? High Islamic culture in Tunisia was purely derivative, a by-product of efforts in Fez or Cairo. It managed to survive because it constantly favored the new over the old, preferred the commentary to the text, and so established a continuity. But it is worth noting that not only Zamakhshari (a late classic writer from central Asia) but also Taftazani and Subki were known and studied, even though their homelands had completely faded from view.

As far as ordinary people were concerned, it seemed as though each region had set about living Islam in its own way. It is astonishing, for example, that the Marabout movements, which were based in the south of Algeria or Morocco, spontaneously sent out a network to the Mediterranean cities of the Maghrib, penetrating areas where the traditions of farthest Asia stubbornly persisted, like a distributary of the great Islamic intellectual tradition. Islam in the Maghrib, whether of the mystical-populist or intellectual-elitist variety, was closed in upon itself, but the same could be said of Islam in India, Iran, or the Arab Mashriq.

It has been suggested that orthodox Islamic urban culture, in this context, spread outwards into the rural world.[3] But one should add that this tide of influence soon began to flow back from the edge of the desert toward the cities. And this phenomenon cannot be explained simply by invoking the constant threat posed by the West. The rebuilding, or rather the creation, of vernacular languages and the taking root of particular political traditions both consummated and manifested the break in Islam before direct aggression had occurred on the part of Europe. But when a later generation examined the *disiecta membra* of the past, it made the surprising discovery that the common cultural heritage had gone on smoldering here and there beneath the ashes, that scholars in Tunis were familiar with Biruni, while those in Lahore studied Sahnun. The *Nahda* was, essentially Arab, but it was an Afghan who set it in motion, a man who was one of the last of the ancients still aware of Islamic ecumenism and one of the first of the moderns. But because the Arabic-speaking world had preserved its language, it found itself in a better position to unearth the ancient patrimony of Islam, to understand it and, ultimately, identify with it.

This identification was not merely linguistic or even cultural in the broad sense. It mirrored the fundamental tension present in classical Islam, which was limited to the Arab world: the sense of a common destiny but of different nations, the search for an ideal model, and finally the gradual emergence of a new culture. Contemporary Arab ideology has become the replica of classical Islam as a historical agent. We are faced with the paradoxical fact that for the first time in history Arab identity is being consciously presented as an end in itself. If it is recapitulating the formal movement of ancient Islam, it is doing so only on a secondary level, since the Islam that constitutes its frame of reference is still living its own life today.

The problem of continuity in Islam as a whole, viewed against the background of discontinuity that we have traced out, lies first of all in its transformations or its syntheses with local cultures, then in the explicit recognition (experienced separately in each region) of an ideal Islam for purposes of orientation, and lastly in the objective survival, more unconscious than conscious, of the tenuous artery of classical culture, especially but not exclusively in the territory that became Arab.

This analysis of a three-tiered continuity underlines the permanence of historical process in the Islamic world and the cardinal importance of the so-called period of decline. This notion of decline, applied to the premodern phase of Islam, makes no sense save as a prelude to death. It has no validity except for an outside observer glancing in retrospect at an extinct civilization. Eighteenth century Muslims had been unaware of this decline until the shock of the encounter with Europe opened their eyes to an evident and utterly unheard of disparity in power. Not that there had not been serious internal strains before, but one may question whether they were part of a general decline or a response to the displacement of Islam's centers of gravity caused by its breakup as a unified historical entity.

If it is true, however, that from the fifteenth century on the rise of Europe and its greed stifled certain Islamic countries, such as Egypt and the Maghrib, it is equally true that the Ottoman Empire maintained its power and prosperity well into the seventeenth century.[4] Under the circumstance we may ask if our historical consciousness may not remain trapped, despite its best efforts, within the confines of its political-cultural environment. In point of fact, Islamic consciousness, as a shaper of future history, had recourse to the concept of decline in order to indict the recent past, while occidental consciousness used it to justify its hegemony: and so in both cases historical thought made itself the servant, or at least the reflection, of concrete needs.

As they faced the increasingly obvious domination by Europe, Muslims felt obliged to rethink their past at the same time as they countered Western ascendancy with steady rejection. But here too the isolated combats they engaged in showed that they were still suffering from their earlier separation. And thus came about the Arab *Nahda* and Arab nationalism, the rebirth of Iran based on Achaemenid tradition, the building of the Kemalist state on a Western model and, conversely, the foundation of Pakistan on strictly Islamic principles. In the meantime Turkestan was swallowed up by Czarist Russia without in the least disturbing a Muslim world that was shattered, nonexistent, a mere geographical expression.

Reviewing the twenty years that followed decolonialization, one looks for some authentic rediscoveries rooted in Islam, but there were none, or very few. Bonds of solidarity were affirmed but only with regard to Afro-Asian (soon to be Third World) ideology. In contrast, in the Cold War years new antagonisms grew up out of the primordial antagonism of that period, between Russia and America. Islam became a tool for political manipulation pure and simple, a kind of bogeyman conjured up by turns against communism and Arab nationalism, just as it could be, and still is, used for the internal goals of political and social conservatism. All sorts of popularizers of Islam never cease to emphasize its collective mobilizing power under the well-worn heading of *Umma*, but this time, paradoxically, it proved to be a rather feeble rallying or defensive principle. There was even less chance of its becoming a positive principle of political unity for the whole Muslim world, despite the quite recent phenomenon of the Islamic renaissance.

It is a clear, conspicuous, indisputable face, however, that Islamic identity, when perceived as the ground of existence, has proved capable of investing tragic moments with the loftiest meaning, at least in certain areas and on the occasions of certain struggles, as in Algeria against French colonialism or in Egypt against Israel. But in such cases of circumscribed conflict—for the fatherland or a given cause—the point was to draw upon a common heritage and not to struggle for the survival of Islam, which was not threatened as a faith, whereas the historical existence of Muslim peoples *was* at stake.

But now the situation is being reversed. The truth is that Islam in the religious sense has never gone so far downhill as it has today, not in quantity—the numbers have increased remarkably—but in quality. In countries with a long Islamic tradition, religious unanimity has been lost, de facto if not *de jure*. Islam is becoming the ideology of the masses, to borrow a term from Gramsci, and less and less the ideology of the political or intellectual elite. If political leaders treat Islam with kid gloves, their motive is evidently fear of cutting themselves off from the masses. The intellectual world is being split into two parts: on one side, the *'ulama* are becoming, once again in the Gramscian sense, traditional intellectuals, enunciating an ideology that is certainly powerful and also favored by the majority but which has increasingly fewer points of contact with the real environment and future projects, an ideology supported largely by the weight of tradition. Modern intellectuals, however, have practically repudiated Islam, whether out of allegiance to Marxism or to modernist ideology and in either case, inspired by Western culture. For the moment, intellectuals belonging to the second category are cut off from the masses, both because of their doctrinal positions and because the powers that be keep them in check or on the run. But they have more influence upon young people than the traditional *ulama* and, despite appearances, on the political world itself.

What Muslim countries lack today is precisely the sort of organic intellectualism once embodied in the *'ulama* of the classical and postclassical epoch. For the most part the modern world has resisted this approach, undoubtedly owing to the intellectualization of politics and the politicization of intellectual life. But a society on the rise must take intellectual control of its own aspirations, however drastically shrunken the magisterium may be by the loss of faith in transcendence and the moral authority that went with it. Pure intellectuality has never existed anywhere, but the illusion of pure intellectuality is nonetheless necessary. So much so that the organic intellectual school could be defined by its power of integration, by the link it forges between past and future history, between the social ideal and the social reality—not a group of ideologues defending a given political order but interpreters of a civilization in process.

## The Problem of Alienation

It may be that Abduh was farther along on the right track than Ziya Gokalp or Lutfi Sayyid. But Islamic reformism represented the most advanced element in the party of traditional intellectuals, just as the secularist or liberal modernism of the colonial era represented the least advanced element in the party of modern intellectuals. The organic intellectuals remained conspicuously absent from the scene because the world in which they evolved was not in charge of its own destiny, hard pressed as it was by a challenge from without, badly met in some places, as well as by seemingly insurmountable inertia from within. All this points up the necessity of steering clear of a double alienation, in the past and in the future. We have already discussed the breakup of the realm of Islamic history, a topic with which analytic thought feels completely at home. Now to the extent that various autonomous regions, Arab-Islamic, Iranian-Islamic, Indo-Islamic, can be built up, organic intellectuals will come forward as active agents of this construction. But this will occur only on condition that they maintain a sense of historical affinity with Islamic sister-cultures, that is, the sense of a shared past brought to life by religion. Just as the grandiose vision of a unified past can never be exalted as the polestar for a Muslim world guided by its own internal movement, so the past, however deeply internalized, cannot be wiped out with a stroke of the pen or reduced to the level of mere tradition.

European civilization was born because barbarian Europe continued to feel nostalgia for the great days of the Empire and carried on the task of rebuilding it. Europe aspired to civilization and realized that aspiration because it would not endure its own barbarism. In the same way the cultural pride of the Arabs drove them irresistibly to reject colonialist domination. They will never duplicate the second century after the Hijra, but they will be able to create a major alternative form of modernity for our time. Muslims believe they have recovered their Islamic identity; the question is, what will come of it? *Not*, assuredly, a new Abbasid empire, but some kind of feeling of solidarity, a rediscovery of values, an examination of self and the world, with a lesson for everyone.

There was a time when Islamic identity was experienced within Islamic space, the *Dar al-Islam*. Now it is lived as a position in history, and as Islamic faith loses ground in society its practice will become more like belonging to one spiritual family among others in a pluralistic context. That is why the problem of alienation is essentially one of historical consciousness and arises most acutely within the area that lays explicit claim to continuity with ancient Islam: the Arab world.

Here, in fact, we observe the paradox that the more distance Arabs put between themselves and the colonialist era, the more they look to outside cultural models. One might even ask whether, despite appearances and beneath the surface, definitive bonds are not now being established with the ancient metropolises, whether a vertical web is not being woven, spanning the planet north to south, whether, in sum, the wave of the future will not move the colonialist countries of Europe toward their old domain, and vice versa. Should that happen, all the major contemporary modes of identity, European, Arab, Islamic, African, and so forth, will come to grief in their most energetic moment of self-affirmation, just as the objective solidarity that grew out of colonialist domination enjoyed a resurgence after suffering the most violent rejection.

Are we talking, then, about alienation or the irresistible evolution of history? Is not alienation in its supreme form the internalizing of the oppressor once direct oppression has stopped, that is, once the victim's defenses have fallen? One may recall the case of Iran, which was converted to Islam after the Arab domination had relaxed its grip and—at least among elite groups—subjected to strong Arab influence for several centuries. It is true that European colonization did not found solid empires, and was consciously rejected as outside oppression in India as in Algeria. But it left behind it the seeds of modernity, nationalism, Marxism and, more concretely, the linguistic or cultural particularity of the dominant metropolis.

Meanwhile, in places where people still cling, on a profound level, to a strong historical identity, after the liveliest cultural reaction proves incapable of eradicating the colonialist culture, the possibility arises of a choice amidst the alienation: the universal message can be preserved while the particularist element is rejected. Iran ended by rejecting the Arabic language and internalizing Islam. It may be that the Maghrib, India, Africa, and Indonesia will one day have the strength to repudiate the languages of Europe while joyfully accepting Europe's universal message. Western-style technology, evidently, is not a universal. Humanism, rationalism, and liberalism are, but they have never been coherently formulated. The Marxist temptation remains, with the enormous questions that it raises. "This is the Islam of modern times," Max Weber declared after the Russian Revolution, no doubt thinking of its all-embracing or egalitarian character, rather than of its domination and identity in the history of nations. But comparisons are odious, and in any case Europe never adopted Marxism as its ideology or deliberately propagated it, as it did liberal values.

The question is, can the cultural alienation brought on by colonialism be overcome without calling for help from that other and more broadly Western form of alienation called Marxism. The fact that colonialism has (for reasons of European ethnocentrism) preserved non-European cultures, that it has been freely rejected by its subjects, that the colonizers themselves turned a deaf ear to the message of the dominated peoples, and finally that there is now a conscious effort afoot to create national or cultural identities—all this suggests that we are dealing with a transitory phenomenon.

For the first time in history a strong, coherent dominating power has been successfully repelled, perhaps because it harbored a fundamental contradiction: it was emanating from a civilization that was centered in itself but behaved like the old-time barbarian conquerors. The purely cultural attraction it had, however, could be exercised only on those sectors that had been deeply affected by colonialism—and that could counterbalance its impact by drawing on either the resources of the past or the cultures of closely related countries with a more solid identity, thanks to their having escaped direct contamination.

The fact remains that this transitional figure, the acculturated intellectual, much more than his counterpart in politics, seems one of the most curious phenomena of contemporary history. At first blush, one might liken such intellectuals to the Hellenistic intellectuals, Egyptian or Syrian, who were cut off from their ethnic world and oriented toward the Hellenistic cultural horizon. But for this comparison to be valid, European culture would have had to vanish from its original home, and the new Alexandrians would have to take it over both in its content and its native languages. Modern intellectuals of this sort are thus not Alexandrians, any more than they are the *mawali* of Europe. Yet there undoubtedly is a temptation to head in that direction: it is found not on the level of creative activity but of lived cultural experience, and it is painful precisely because it is semialienation.

## THE ARAB NATION: GENESIS AND DEVELOPMENT

Islam broke down as a dynamically organized totality, especially in politics, well before the imperialistic intrusion of Europe. This breakdown, however, was not a straightforward process. For that to be the case, each national region of Islam would have had to spell out a positive identity for itself. This task began in the Arab world at the beginning of the nineteenth century. But though it went off relatively smoothly everywhere else, giving rise to nations that were ordinary, uncomplicated affairs (nations first and then, in addition, Muslim), the Arabs had a hard time of it. More than any other area, the Arab world has captured the underlying thrust of Islamic history. Hence the Arab nation could never be a nation of the usual sort, defined by its particularities. It is a unitary tension, a dialectic between nation in the broad and narrow senses, a history still in gestation.[5]

The word *nation* is supposed to translate the Arabic *Umma*, which Orientalists used to render as "community" when the Islamic *Umma* was under discussion. It is clear that contemporary Arabs now give various national, patriotic, and political meanings to the old concept of *Umma*. But we cannot say that *Umma arabiyya* and "Arab nation" are equivalent, since each phrase carries the burden of a very different historical experience. The French (or English) word *nation* originally had a distinctive rather than a synthetic tenor. Within a given framework (for example, the kingdom of France), it denoted regional communities (the Norman, Picard, etc., nations). For the outside world it served all through the modern era as a name for the mercantile communities together with their consuls. So it had, in this case, an inter-European significance based on the unity engendered by a civilization vis-à-vis the other—such as Muslims. It is scarcely necessary to recall the unifying effect of the French Revolution and, in particular, the way it affirmed the nation both as an internal reality and as the foundation of political sovereignty.

European nations came to self-awareness in the nineteenth century, when the principle of nationality, though resisted by the multinational empires, was becoming the much-heralded basis of Europe's internal organization. The First World War gave a practical demonstration of this principle, especially by putting forth the nation as an exalted value and ideal, with the results that we all know. Nevertheless, if nationalism reached its zenith between the two world wars, the European nations had been slowly developing ever since the foundation of the barbarian kingdoms, in the sense that the establishment of separate political frameworks strongly accentuated the differences between peoples. Protected by such frameworks, distinct languages emerged and then crystallized. There we have a rapid survey of the historical European experience of nationhood.

One wonders to what extent the European concept of the nation, a feature so peculiar to the history of Europe, has been exported, along with other indigenous creations, beyond European borders. How much of it, for example, did the Arabs borrow in order to construct both their different nation-states (Egypt, Algeria, Syria . . .) and their ideology of the great unitary Arab nation? The fact is that at the heart of Arab reality some assimilation of the European system has undoubtedly occurred, but specific historical experiences carry just as much weight.

*The Arab Nation and Arab Countries in History*

It is difficult to speak of the Arab nation on the eve of the appearance of Islam, but we can speak of an Arab world as endowed with a certain cultural identity and constituted by Arabia (the interior) and the diaspora in Syria and Mesopotamia. Islam founded the *Umma*, a structure of political-religious solidarity, which bit by bit absorbed the whole fabric of Arab life, both inside and outside.

Under the orthodox Caliphate, just as with the Umayyads, the *Umma* could defined as the Arab-Islamic nation, that is, at once Arab and Islamic. The non-Muslim Arab minorities were excluded from this nation, as well as, obviously, the majority of the subject peoples that made up the Empire, for the Umayyad Empire was dominated by the Arabs, and their ideology was Islam. As for the conquered peoples—Egyptians, Persians, Berbers, Aramaeans from Iraq, Kurds, Turks—they were neither Arab nor, for the most part, Muslim.

It was in the late Abbasid period, after the tenth century, and precisely on account of the fragmentation of the Empire, that the process of Islamicizing and Arabicizing outsiders, which had already begun to take shape during the great Abbasid epoch (seventh to ninth century) was consolidated and amplified. But we must not confuse the two features of this campaign. Persia and its traditional cultural hinterland (central Asia, northern India) adopted Islam but not Arabic. On the contrary, the greater part of the former Byzantine territories, along with Iraq, adopted both Islam and Arabic at the same time, but by a rapid and total, the popular acceptance of Arabic at the base did not extend to all levels of society. In any case, an important phenomenon occurred (just when is hard to determine, but doubtless after the eleventh century): the profound penetration of Arabic into what are now the Arab countries, and the rejection of the Arabic implant in the Iranian world and its successors (the Ottoman Empire, for example). Nevertheless Arabic long remained, among the Iranians and Turks, the language of the cultured elite and it is the language of worship to this day. It is important to note that this radical evolution was purely objective, with no implications for the consciousness of the people affected. In the centuries that witnessed the birth and development of the European nations—from the fifteenth to the eighteenth century—what, in fact, was happening in the Muslim world?

First, the ideal of a unitary Islam, corresponding to the ancient *Umma*, was maintained.

Second, there was a de facto breakup of Islam, in the sense that cultural, commercial, human and, of course, political ties were seriously weakened, if not torn apart. This fragmentation was not offset by a new system built along geographical or linguistic lines. Instead there arose an artificial arrangement based on the various Muslim empires. In other words, if the bonds between, say, the Safavid Persians and the Maghribans were completely broken, there was scarcely more evidence of unity among the Maghribans themselves or between Egyptians and Iraqis, or Iraqis and Tunisians, though they spoke the same language. The Ottoman Empire, having subjugated almost the entire Arabic-speaking world, failed to establish anything more than bilateral connections between each province and the metropolis. As time went on, this double split progressively deepened, until it reached its nadir in the first thirty years of the nineteenth century.

Third, this did not prevent each major region from living Islam in its own way, in matters of both high culture and religion. And such autonomy was a determining factor in the way Muslim countries built up their own vernacular languages, local

civilizations, and traditions of government. It goes without saying that, within the territory that later developed into today's
Arab world, there was no awareness of any solidarity grounded
in race, culture, language, or tradition. It is likewise apparent that
serious nation-building took place insofar as each country was
free from Ottoman domination. Morocco, Tunisia, Egypt, the
parts of Arabia not under Ottoman control (Nejd, Yemen) proved
to have a more solid national tradition than did Algeria, Syria-
Palestine, or Iraq. But the Ottoman hegemony does not by itself
explain this dissimilarity; we must also consider the different
patterns of evolution during that obscure but crucial period from
the eleventh to the fifteenth century, when Iraq was living in, for
all intents and purposes, absolute void, while Mamluk Egypt
enjoyed an epoch of remarkably good organization.

In conclusion, I would say that at least until 1850 and probably up until the establishment of direct colonial regimes (the
last two decades of the nineteenth century) there was neither a
unitary Arab consciousness embracing the Arabic-speaking
world, from the Atlantic Ocean to the Persian Gulf, nor partial
Arab consciousness embracing one or two countries, nor even a
generalized patriotic consciousness in the more politically so-
phisticated states. But then, in a noteworthy moment, the dawn
of the twentieth century saw the simultaneous arrival of both
unitary feeling and a more restricted patriotic awareness, and
complementing rather than opposing one another. With that in
mind, it must be reaffirmed that, in the depths of reality and at
the end of the long evolution that has been traced, the presence
of the latent objective structures that made such a development
possible can be found.

*Development of the Unitary Consciousness and the Patriotic
Consciousness*

It must be acknowledged that the cultural phenomenon of
the *Nahda* (renaissance) paved the way for both these forms of
development by reconstructing the Arab heritage, by restoring
the connection to the splendors of an age now given classic

status, in a word, by spreading an atmosphere and ideology of renascence. The immediate consequence of this movement, whose vital center lay in Egypt and Syria, was the emergence of a modern Arabic language and literature, hence a re-Arabization by the core of the Middle East.

This re-Arabization, which was gradually extended to the peripheral areas as well as to every layer of society, was at once fostered and thwarted by Western colonialization or at least by Western influence. For Arabic-speaking Christians, there was also the desire to throw off the Turkish yoke, which did not weight quite so heavily on the Muslim majority. The unitary national ideology, whose purposes were fundamentally political, took over from the *Nahda* and made use of its gains, but it was a different sort of thing. Significantly enough, it won a permanent place for itself during the First World War, in the regions directly dominated by the Ottoman Empire (the Fertile Crescent). Perhaps it was anti-Turkish, but it was not anti-Ottoman because, up until 1908, the Hamidian Empire had, to a certain degree, propagated a pan-Ottoman ideology that brought together people of various nationalities (Turks, Arabs, etc.). For their part, the English encouraged the Arabs to regroup in a distinct kingdom encompassing Arabia, Syria-Palestine, and Iraq. And so in all sorts of ways foreign relations turned out to be critically important in the formation of a modern Arab *political* consciousness; that is, destined to take shape in a political structure transcending the old administrative divisions. To a great extent France caused the failure of this attempt to regroup, just as England, less than a hundred years before, had stopped cold efforts to unify the Arab Levant under the rule of Muhammad Ali.

The failure of this sort of regional system on an Arab base did not prevent the Arab world from structuring itself into states, from organizing itself, affirming itself politically, and experiencing a relative autonomy. Dominated by Westerners, the states of the Maghrib nonetheless enjoyed a kind of formal independence in between the world wars. From then on, the West would be the exclusive target of the struggles organized both to build the Arab nation and to win national liberation in each country—with the second type of struggle clearly playing the larger role. As the struggles for partial liberation intensified, however, the dialectical link between nation-building and liberation was strengthened accordingly. One was no less a Syrian, an Iraqi, or a Tunisian for thinking of oneself as an Arab and a Muslim, quite the contrary. And the modern (for the 1930s) means of diffusing information (schools, newspapers, books, radio), by discussing cultural re-Arabization in depth, contributed equally to the advance of the nationalist movements and to the reinforcement of inter-Arab solidarity. In all this the irruption of the masses onto the historical scene had a decisive impact.

Nothing illustrates this dialectical reciprocity better than the postwar era, which witnessed simultaneously:

1. The liberation of the Maghrib and its spectacular entry into the Arab sphere;

2. The first stirrings of the Palestinian problem, which powerfully crystallized unitary feeling;

3. The appearance of Nasserism, which converted Egypt to the idea of Arab renewal, developed the passion for unity in the Arab masses and, not satisfied with linking it to a certain number of goals (a quest for dignity and independence, social radicalism, solidarity with the Third World), actually took some concrete steps toward unification—none of which had lasting success;

4. Elaboration of the Baathist doctrine and the reorganization of Syria and Iraq under its aegis.

The 1960s witnessed the strongest development to date of the unitary ideology by means of its two contrasting sources, Nasserist and Baathist. Unitary action before the defeat of 1967 was aggressive, exclusionary, triumphalist, given to setting off one part of the Arab world against another. Since 1967, however, there have been signs of Arab unanimity, of a restructuring of Arab consciousness beyond the limits of particular politicosocial regimes: the entire Arab world, by making the Palestinian question its special cause, presented a de facto unitary front toward the outside world, just when schemes for aggressive unification were being abandoned.

The upshot is that today, in the post-Nasser period, unitary ideology has lost ground as a political theory, but the Arab world is doing a better job of organizing exchanges within and concerted action without, and it appears, vis-à-vis outsiders, as a coherent partnership, a homogeneous and already nearly unified force. The particular states that have reemerged into history, however, are also taking form, solidifying, and building themselves up from within. To a large extent, present-day collective Arab sensibility, especially in the Mashriq, has ratified the gains of a hundred years of *Nahda* and the unitary vision. But to an equally large extent the myth of a powerful, unified, centralized Arab nation-state, identifying with the glory of the first Arabs, now lies in shambles, except in Khadafi's romantic vision. Yet the problem for the future is how to evaluate this ambivalent situation not in terms of failure, not by clothing it in voluntarist language, but rather in a dialectical formulation: at once as a living, contradictory dynamic and as a process steadily building its truth.

*Future Perspectives*

The Arab nation today is a cultural nation, just as the *Umma* was a religious nation. It is not political in the sense that it is headed by a state power structure, but in the sense that it confronts the outside world by affirming itself as a closely integrated, indissoluble, quasi-mystical fellowship, profoundly conscious of having a single destiny. It is the superstructure overshadowing the nation-states and conferring on them a presence in the world, a place in universal history, and a certain greatness.

Arabs must, in a word, work out a doctrine of double loyalty and organize the future as a function of the present. Arab consciousness must maintain its normal level of intensity, but it would not be healthy to pin all hopes on achieving some sort of absolute unity. Just as ecumenical Arab consciousness ought to be treated as sacrosanct, so the concrete efforts in its behalf ought to be flexible, empirical, pragmatic. What would such a policy imply?

If worse came to worst, the self-realization of the Arab nation as a political entity might never come about. But all would be lost if an ideology of the nation-state in the narrow sense (greater Arabia, greater Algeria, greater Egypt, for example) should appear and spread. A simplification of the Arab political map would certainly be desirable, and it would certainly be hard to deny the existence of major powers, as well as that of artificial or nonviable states, within the Arab world. But, as I see it, any policy of state power to be deployed within the Arab sphere would not only be dangerous but doomed to failure; because, as everyone knows, those internal powers are built on sand. And the fragmentary power aimed at would be no more than a subpower on the international scene.

At bottom, but in a more serious vein, what the unitary ideology is aiming at is the power provided by a large state with clear objectives and concentrated instruments of coercion. Yet I, as an Arab, can scarcely entertain the notion that America, Europe, or Russia would allow so cohesive a unit to be founded in the heart of the Old World—apart from the internal difficulties already mentioned. So it would take a truly fantastic burst of energy for a creation like this to establish itself and survive: a unique degree of enthusiasm would be called for, or else a historic outbreak of violence, which would be unthinkable without a revolutionary campaign of conquest. In the latter case, if they wished to unite, Arabs ought first to hate each other, split into conflicting groups, and get into the infernal game of excommunication—a return to the old *odium theologicum*.

The present situation offers what is emphatically the most promising point of departure. The work of the various Muslim states should continue to concentrate on their own environments: economic, academic, institutional, and social. They should build the practical structures with the attention to detail that no large state could match. But political regimes should give a uniform shape to their institutions, even while intensify-ing real exchanges. Because if the two levels—on the one hand, the cultural mystique and lofty foreign policy (the only ways in which the Arab nation exists today) and, on the other, the material structures—do not bond together, there will be no dialectic, just a schizoid and wretched reality.

Still, development can always occur, and it can and must be nourished by the happy accident of oil revenues. Today oil accentuates differences, it runs counter to unity. Tomorrow it will provide a good basis for both development and unity if, once a tragic age has given way to an age of pioneering, the Arab nation, with ardor and stubborn effort, commits itself to the path of empirical yet rational relativism, not by abandoning its vision of the absolute, but in order to serve it.

# 7

# Europe as a Particular Case

Europe as a historical agent presents itself in the paradoxical guise of a force at once composite and powerfully original. It drew from diverse sources (classical antiquity, German culture, Christianity), and this has led it to break away, now from one, now from another, to affirm itself, throughout a series of continuing transformations, as a movement, as a conquest, and as a self unmaking and remaking itself. Thanks to the fact that it showed humble respect for an idealized antiquity and a Christianity thrust upon it, Europe was able to surpass the one and maintain a distance from the other. As a supremely assimilative and creative entity, unstable, paradoxical, and dialectical in the extreme, Europe has never really known quiet or repose, a "smooth" history, or what might be called an existence without history.

As old as Islam, it inherited an ancient cultural foundation, an ancient political ideal, and an ancient religion, all of which were superimposed on new nations. With Islam, in contrast, a new element was grafted on to ancient peoples. In speaking of Islam, we can use terms such as necessity, voluntarism, unitary thinking, synthesis, and passion for continuity, whereas for Europe we would have to speak of contingency and surrender to the unforeseen, of internal divisions, exclusion, and a passion for breaking away. Never having subordinated its existence to a single explicit principle, Europe never identified itself with one, preferred becoming over being, motion over stability, its creations over its personality. Every movement within the body of Europe denied the other but integrated it into itself. None of them proved capable of carrying the day all by itself without regrets, retrieval of losses, or returns to the past. Europe's origins were diverse, and so were the changes that it managed to admit, internalize, direct and, for a time, stabilize. So there was a break, but there was integration too and, it could be argued, a certain continuity.

In fact, just as the Germanic invasions did not wholly erase antiquity, neither did the Renaissance suppress the Middle Ages at a stroke, and the French Revolution ran in tandem with the Industrial Revolution almost without being aware of it. There was no radical, conscious, deliberate, enduring break, of the sort that justifies the claim, at the end of the line, that a civilization, a culture, a religion, or any given world with its network of meanings, is finished. Europe's historical consciousness feels and postulates a temporal continuity, from the Germanic invasions onward, and the line of descent from Rome is objectively clear. The Romanesque churches and Gothic cathedrals dotting the landscape of Europe are not some sort of strange monuments built by forgotten peoples. Christianity may be dying, but it is not dead. And the Papacy, an institution nearly two thousand years old, is still on its feet.

I am not speaking here of deep, underlying material or spiritual structures, of permanently established patterns. The issue at stake is a conscious cultural continuity: although Europe bestows a privileged status on its modern face, it still recognizes itself in the totality of its history, so that it does not view the Middle Ages the way Islam views the ancient Near East or Ptolemaic Egypt. For its part, Islam inflicted an ideological break in the historical awareness of the East, for example by erasing Pharaonic Egypt from the memory of the Egyptian people—until it emerged once again from its long night, after being unearthed by European archaeology. Hence there can be no question of denying the cultural foundations of European identity, but the avatars of that identity compel us to define it less by any specific content than by a kind of leap connected to creative effort, a leap that precedes the break but that incorporates it within itself as it moves ahead.

## BEING AND CIVILIZATION

There can be no disputing the fact that modernity is the dominant influence on Europe's destiny, but it is not the only one. It committed Europe to the path of an exceptionally productive enterprise, of short duration but great historical significance. Yet it should be noted that the Renaissance (a *re*-birth), together with a religious reform, presided over the installation of the new European civilization. This Renaissance, at once the continuation and the antithesis of what went before, first appeared in the land most deeply impregnated with the traditions of antiquity, the place where their rediscovery was easiest: Italy. Modern Europe in its first manifestation was shaped and educated by its Mediterranean regions, the very zone where contact with two great but different civilizations, classic and Islamic, was experienced most forcefully. In this way continuity presented itself as the primordial element in the operation of breaking away—just the opening up to the outside world, which occurred at the same time, turned out to be essential for stimulating internal creativity.

Through a sense of continuity and deliberate imitation, an intercultural transmission occurred; through the mediation of ancient sculpture, of Greek thought, of Arab science and technology, Europe felt a surge of intellectual ambition. A new mental climate appeared, along with fresh aspirations and, finally, a desire to emulate the greatest cultures of the past and in so doing to achieve self-realization. Just as Christopher Columbus discovered America while searching for the Indies, all of Europe, enthusiastically seeking out ancient art and Arab science, founded European culture and science. But if modern Europe identified both with its new spirit and its creative accomplishments, Europe as a whole would be defined by its remarkable aptitude for reshaping itself through self-repudiation.

European creative energies, in their boundless fecundity, were at bottom more a matter of development than of pure creation. Europe invented neither science nor music nor philosophy nor technology, but it developed them to unheard of levels, clothing them with seriousness and truth. We have seen that if Europe effected a gigantic change, this change has in turn left its mark on its inner substance. We may admire in passing Europe's brave willingness, on its own initiative, to take risks and call itself into question, but the problem remains as always why its achievements were so sudden, so unexpected and, as we know now, a model for all of humanity.

Hegel found a dialectical explanation for this in the idea that beneath a layer of barbarism were two fruitful principles (Germanic thought and Christianity), which had an explosive and (belatedly) productive encounter. But if we postulate a historical continuity with Rome, the data look altogether different, and they raise another question: Why did it take so many centuries for Europe to find its way, to elaborate its classical norms, to burst forth with its potent civilization, its intellectual and artistic vigor? Because the triumph of the barbarian invasions meant a breakdown of Mediterranean civilization, which was brutally cut off from its eastern roots. Pushed toward the north, a new, inarticulate Europe began rebuilding over a void, whereas Islam fell heir to an eastern empire that had been strongly organized by the Persians.

The truth is that there were many renaissances, from the Carolingian era on down, because old Roman Europe had never resigned itself to the fact that it had passed, or left behind, its barbarianism. A civilization in any given region can be destroyed, but not the idea of civilization. The depth of that barbarianism explains both the delay of Europe's success and its unique quality once it came. For, if the delay had been quickly made up, it would have been followed by a brilliant civilization, but not by a revolution with universal implications. This is the paradox of European civilization.

The dialectical power of Europe grows out of the composite character of its origins, as well as from this paradox of civilization. And the cost of that power has been an essential instability, an infidelity to itself, and a sort of mutilation. The effort expended on its achievements was great but not unprecedented in history. The thesis of Promethean exceptionalism has to be rejected: even if it had existed, this Promethean spirit would be evidence of nothing more than the barbarian stock onto which a passion for civilization had been grafted.

Europe's success is explained not by a great spurt of energy, but by its new orientation, its shifting of goals: the way it directed mind toward matter, progressively chose this world over, or by means of, the world beyond (Weber), and localized the absolute in the depths of the self. This success is fatefully recorded in such basic choices, but for civilizations dedicated to essence or permanence this sort of choice never took place and, objectively speaking, it is arbitrary and thus relative. If for a "spiritually minded" Muslim or even Christian, the world is nothing, any worldly undertaking is empty or devoid of interest. Islam was familiar with both the temptation to rationalism and the love of the world, but its leaders constantly preferred the cohesion of essence to the need for rationality and perhaps they were driven to this option. When all of Asia denigrated Europe's frenzied development, taxing it as materialistic, this was no mere outburst of bitterness. In a profound sense the essentialist civilizations were accusing Western civilization of diluting its essence for the sake of its activity, and making others pay the price of their fidelity to themselves.

In reality, what the Muslims—among other peoples—failed to realize was that Europe had not abdicated its spirituality but displaced it, that its (quite real) materialism was rooted in an adventure of the mind. Though it abandoned its own religion and stripped others of theirs, Europe did not plunge into licentiousness, madness, or gross vulgarity. Rather it made science over into a new form of prayer, with its own ascetical practices, demands for self-denial, and so forth. The scholar was not a libertine, but a hero of the mind, as the saint was a hero of the soul.

## HISTORY AND CIVILIZATION

This European civilization, with its choices and exclusions, with its ideology of progress, its humanism, and its transvaluation of the values on which humanity had lived until then, constituted a revolution in world history and, as such, one of the great moments in the human adventure. This was Civilization, as proud, imperial-trivial nineteenth-century Europe called it, demeaning everything non-European with an insensitivity that I still find impossible to explain. (Was it triumphalism, lack of experience, a parvenu spirit, and too abrupt an entrance into the wider field of human civilization?)

From a stricter standpoint, European civilization as a way of life or particular mode of existence appears to have had a commonplace brilliance, but no more. It shone over all of western Europe, which it unified in its primitive phase, in its medieval period, or during its splendid time of flowering, from the sixteenth to the nineteenth century. Because Europe was politically divided from the beginning (whence the dramatic character of its history), and it lived in the shadow of a unifying civilization, it owed some of its richness to this multipolarity, as Hume clearly saw.

But Europe did not become aware of how original its civilization was until it compared it with that of others: with the Moriscos in sixteenth-century Spain, with the Turks on its eastern fringes, at the time of the great voyages of discovery, and finally after the colonial expansion of the nineteenth century. Then the internal disparities faded from view and the white man affirmed himself and closed ranks in solidarity against everything outside. Europeans have never been united except against somebody. History and civilization have taken divergent or parallel paths, with civilization remaining helpless to calm the tumult of an unsettled and fundamentally domestic history. Owing to the fact that, despite all the foreign expansion, Europeans have always regarded history as internal history, European civilization never unified hearts, concentrating instead on itself and developing its own potentialities. It was just as insular as European history, not that it borrowed much from its contemporaries: it borrowed their instruments, but almost never their spirit, their color, or any sort of tonality. Nothing is so moving as to see a desire for refinement slowly emerging—it reached its culmination in the eighteenth century, under the aegis of the aristocracy—from the uncouthness of the Middle Ages. It was then that the decor of life in society was now fixed. The bourgeois civilization that followed, after the Industrial Revolution, would have been extremely flat, if it had not internalized the visions of the aristocracy.

There is no doubt, however, that civilization in the strict sense remains Europe's weak point because of its banality and lack of greatness. It cannot boast of any superiority over other civilizations, Islamic, Indian, Chinese, and so forth, except on account of its peculiar ethos (as opposed to its achievements): its sense of freedom, its distance from the irrational weight of tradition, the intimate link that it established with a lofty cultural aspiration. This happened precisely because it was a new civilization, but not all new civilizations have worshiped culture as the European kind did.

Because it was not undergirded by a compact empire, European civilization today suffers from a lack of greatness, and in the past it was seldom aware of its unity. Because it infiltrated so many states and nations, it penetrated the deepest levels of the social world, and went through an infinite number of variations. But one must remember, to the extent that it was willy-nilly associated with a new spirit—one that transcended it, to be sure—it wished to be, whether or not it succeeded, broadly human, the most consciously human of civilizations. Singularly inventive, complex, diversified, active, even vitalistic, prizing individual destiny and so favoring an intense existence over a harmonious one, and progress over equilibrium, this civilization seems lacerated, constantly stricken with a bad conscience. Urged on by the dream of perfecting the human condition, it ran aground on the shore of the greatest perversions in history. It was as if civilization, being a projection of instinct rather than its negation, was forever crashing into the hard facts of human

evil. All civilizations are built upon injustice, most have been at
once for humanity and against it. But this one, which explicitly
endeavored to serve man, found its limits in man himself. And
so once again we see the crucial necessity of separating the
message, the aspirations, the horizon of European civilization
from its lived reality. This gap amplified the tragedy of the West
as much as it expresses its grandeur.

## The Decline of Culture: Its New Look

Thus the humanist ideal ended in tragedy, and with it faded
the central political role of Europe (in the geographic sense, at
least). Much more important than this, however, was the breakdown of cultural creativity. Ever since the First World War,
European thinkers had begun to wonder about the ultimate
purpose and values of their culture, thereby creating a culture at
one remove, critical, questioning, anxious. But predicting the
''decline of the West'' is not enough to stop its downward slide,
and it is perfectly futile to turn this increased awareness into
further grounds for pride. Because that implies a belief, not in
pessimism, but in the illusion that European culture has a vocation to perpetual renewal. Foucault makes a good case for the
end of man as an object of knowledge, but he exalts the new
formalism of structure as the hope and future of Western culture, rejecting any notion that its content might be exhausted.

But the scientific study of culture, the refinements of art or
analysis, only serve to throw into sharp relief both the naivety
of the past and its high-spirited greatness. For whereas the
ancestors generated new life, laid foundations, opened up
original vistas, the epigones write footnotes, repeat the past,
spin around in pure negation. We may argue over whether
Michelet was naive, Weber too much given to rough generalizations, or Freud simply inadequate, but it matters little:
neither the *Annales* school nor American sociologists nor the
neo-Freudians can measure up to them. Michelet shaped the
historical consciousness of an entire nation, Weber founded

European sociology, and Freud created psychoanalysis—all of them, it should be added, with the help of their many predecessors, at the cost of long sufferings and struggles, with feverish efforts and strong-minded faith.

Everything then lay waiting to be discovered, and now this culture finds everything already accomplished. And the frenetic attempts by our contemporaries to mimic renewal or to refine old positions simply hasten the ossification of European culture and ultimately make the past still more moving. Descartes's loneliness *was* moving, Voltaire's hypochondriac exile was derisively tragic, and Balzac's ordered jumble still can move us. But the great innovative figures did not go looking for a malediction in order to be creative. Their agony was thrust upon them because they wanted a new kind of thought, a new life, a new art. Taine was quite unjust to see nothing more in the eighteenth-century *philosophes* than deeply flawed ordinary men.[1] Michelet, who was a child of the Revolution, recognized their paternal role with a fine, incisive phrase, calling them "the precursors" and the "masters of the Revolution."[2] Europe today smiles at the follies of the Revolution, but without Voltaire there would have been no Sartre and, without Voltaire's years of exile, no immunity for Sartre.

It is significant that Foucault began by particularizing European culture, so as to proceed to a historical or, to use his term, "archaeological" examination. Twenty years earlier a gifted French philosopher would commit himself to a sui generis tradition and follow its course. This kind of self-reflection is a sign that a culture's work is finished.

But the humanist point of view no longer saves the situation: Humanism insists too harshly on defending the exemplary character of Europe's message. We see this pattern everywhere, but it comes as more of a jolt to find it in the books of one of Europe's most universal minds, André Malraux. Not only did Malraux's evolution, from *La Tentation de l'Occident* to the afterword in *Les Conquérants*, lead him to political nationalism and cultural Eurocentrism, but all his writings clearly show the effect of an implicit belief that Western culture has reached the

highest level of consciousness and that in his transhistoric survey of art the heritage of all previous cultures crumbles to
pieces. When the non-European world experienced a resurrection, Malraux just stayed away. When it spoke with its own
voice, he fell silent.

The recent publication of Husserl's *Krisis* shows how, beneath the universalism of the philosophical tradition, the old
idea is still going strong, that Europe represents humanity in its
rational, self-conscious mode. More bitterness comes out here,
and a highly significant defensive posture, with an intuition
that the twilight of reason and values has arrived. In its encounters with the other, of course, European humanism has
proved that it can challenge itself. But self-criticism is often a
flimsy disguise for an ambiguous self-glorification, a nostalgia
for what have been determined a priori to be Europe's truthful
values; in a word, for a certain moral-cultural fundamentalism.

An archaeological vision of culture, formalism, ambiguity,
the harshness of humanism, the pride of the philosophical
tradition: this is the end of a world, an event pointed out with
still greater clarity by the drying up of creativity. When art seeks
nothing beyond itself, and then seeks its own destruction, when
learning becomes institutionalized so as to take a marginal position, when the intelligentsia turns into mere commentators,
when culture is transformed from the matrix of society into its
methodically staged spectacle, then we can truly say that its
cultural greatness is finished.

This is not to ignore the comebacks, the occasional brilliant
strokes, and the vitalizing migration to America, Europe's cultural daughter. Yet, even though these terms—end, decline,
twilight, ossification—derive from a picture of the West as facile
as it is old-fashioned, and in spite of the sharper awareness
today, compared with the naive views of the recent past, there is
a prevailing impression that an irremediable loss of substance
has occurred. Western culture can always discover new material
to work with, but that is not where its problem lies. It has been
hurt most of all by a loss of elasticity, a drop in its level of
aspiration; it has been undermined by the ideology of immediate

happiness. A great passion has been snuffed out, never to be rekindled. The whole issue, then, is this: what might Europe bequeath to future cultures, how much of its legacy is transferable, and how much will be its secret, buried forever in the depths of its specificity?

## The Essence of Western Culture

The old European culture—from the sixteenth century to 1950—was eager to make new discoveries, was enthusiastic, creative, and critical. It was impassioned for the truth, penetrated with a thirst for the absolute that we can discern as readily in its instrumental music as in its literature, painting, philosophy, or science. The value of Western culture lies in its successful conjunction of a sense of the absolute and a sense of man. At least that is how this culture saw itself, because naturally the outsider cannot get past its surface, except through initiation or apprenticeship. To a Muslim anchored in his own world, a Beethoven piano concerto seems cacophonous; we know that to Chinese ears, Western music sounded like a sort of march. And it is true that instrumental music expresses the European bent for energetic affirmation—the thunderous roar of a barely transcended barbarism. But it managed to wrest from the human heart its deepest inwardness, its most intense share of the absolute.

What distinguishes Western music from other kinds is not polyphony, since a genuine classicism exists in oriental monophonic music, but the moments of sadness and nostalgia that it has captured in chamber music and the sonata through an act of pure personal creativity. Each musical piece is thus a composition, the work of a man and of a certain solitude, not the labor of a tradition drawing upon itself. This principle can likewise be discerned in painting, although during the period under discussion music was the most elevated and characteristically European of the arts, attracting to itself all the lines of force of the European genius.

Why, beginning with the quattrocentro, did the act of painting acquire meaning and value as an outstanding act of civilization rather than of religion? And why did an exercise that elsewhere might be considered futile or merely aesthetic take it
upon itself to express a vision of the world, a new passion, a
journey of the mind? This is the real problem, as opposed to
knowing whether Europe was capable of inventing perspective
or chiaroscuro all by itself. Some Iranian Islamic miniaturists
had tried to express the mystical élan of the Muslim soul by the
very negation of perspective and of realistic images altogether.[3]
But Muslim mysticism, though quite superior to all other varie-
ties, basically expressed itself in poetry and in action, whereas
Rembrandt was one of the great mystics of Europe. European
painting harbored a wish to interpret and surpass reality, it was
a projection on canvas of the artist's ego as well as incomparable
historical testimony: a reading of the world and of history,
straightforward, unconscious, powerful.

The intertwining of the self, the absolute, and history—the
central configuration of European culture—is given a self-
conscious, theoretically articulated form in philosophy, one of
the greatest achievements of the European mind. Great not
because it reached higher levels of rationality than Greek or
Arab thought in the conceptual instruments it fashioned, but
because it linked the rationality and inner music of the West.
The central core of philosophy is idealism, where the ego becomes the organizer and practically the creator of the world.
Nothing could be stranger or more fascinating than metaphysical idealism as we see it in Berkeley, Leibniz, Kant, Fichte,
Hegel, Husserl, Heidegger, Sartre, and Merleau-Ponty. It is a
true poem of consciousness at grips with the world—meaning
by the world neither the secular realm nor the universe, but
everything that is set over against consciousness and that consciousness creates, orders, establishes, or gives value to.

What is the world? It has neither history nor its own tempo-
rality, but is born with each consciousness and dies with it. It is
the adventure of a life that projects its beam on an unknowable
space which exists outside of it and, with it, becomes a world,

emerging from its bottomless obscurity. All of modern Western philosophy revolves around the world and mind. It is profoundly opposed to science although, paradoxically, it aspired to lay the groundwork of science, which on its highest levels continues the work of philosophy. Why was a man like Kant haunted by the perfection of mathematics and later by the efficiency of physics when his whole teaching and in particular his categories of space and time surreptitiously introduced the supremacy of consciousness? As he grew older, Kant himself made his way toward an extremely interesting cosmology, which was something altogether different from science in the scholarly sense.[4] What is left then to serve as horizon and foundation of this metaphysics except the idea of death? As authentic as its quest for the truth may have been, it resolves nothing and simply gives an account of our destiny. And were one to believe it in all its implications, to live and internalize it, such a *Weltanschauung* would logically issue in a sort of madness, precisely to the extent that it dissolves the naive vision of the world, with its stability and legitimacy.

Of course, there are degrees of idealism—which is not the same thing as solipsism—but they all exalt the ego and the sovereignty of consciousness at every step of the way: that is the essential aim of the old metaphysics, of ontology and phenomenology. Significantly enough, Hegel, who meditated on the whole range of being, was led to explore the depths of consciousness. He recognized, moreover, the Fichtean idealism of the Ego as the necessary intellectual manifestation of the man of reason, or of postreligious European man. What shall we say of Husserl and his vigorous reaffirmation of the transcendental Ego, which he places at the heart of the Western tradition since Plato,[5] so emphatically that one critic has spoken of a "paranoia of the Ego"?[6] It may be that the final moments of European philosophy are being spent on a gigantic effort at reconnoitering the outside world—gigantic because it is headed exactly counter to the entire philosophical tradition, whose extinction it signals. One of the last documents of Western philosophy, the posthumous work of Merleau-Ponty, left poignantly unfinished and sounding like a last will and testament, was a supreme attempt at reconciliation with the sensible world.[7]

In its finest achievements, European philosophy, which was the offshoot of Franco-German cooperation,[8] with the Germans predominating, did not assume an Absolute. It claimed to be a *search* for absolute truth, at once humble and wildly ambitious. Humble because it had only the most ordinary tools at its disposal: the world as perceived and unanalyzed, consciousness, the body. It has to be compared with Muslim mysticism, itself inspired by Platonism, in that it sought the truth of the Absolute in the depths of the self. But at this point the comparison breaks down, because the world is absent from Muslim mysticism, whereas in Western philosophy the ultimate reality is the fleeting gestalt of world-and-self that tirelessly creates and re-creates itself in intersubjectivity. For the West, truth is a matter of rational progression; for Islam, truth unveils itself by the path of illumination, like the dawn of day—*Ishraq*. Were it not for that approach, Western philosophy would be no more than a vast and splendid poem. But its strangeness is nonetheless evident, reminding us that every high culture has a strong esoteric component. However rational it would like to be, it remains the prisoner of its spiritual lineage, of its own tradition, but also of the ground swells that issue from the collective soul.

Tradition shapes our longings with its discipline, but in all the branches of culture those longings go beyond tradition. Not just philosophy but the whole of Western culture was idealist in the sense that it bound up subjectivity with a spiritual ambition. One of the illusions of that ambition, thus defined, has been the glorifying of action by men of culture. We are familiar with the myth of the lonely navigator, more powerful today than it ever was before. Even philosophy has managed to cultivate the other, nonidealist side of the Western psyche, the call to action. Spengler sees this as the distinctive feature of Europe's philosophical passion. He invokes Schelling, Schopenhauer, and Nietzsche. He might well have referred to Hegel's dictum that "The true being of man is his action." And later, as we know, Sartre would identify man with his activity and his "project."

But what is all this except the moral decline of philosophy which, when it ceases to be philosophy, starts becoming the exalted self-image of a real, expanding society, and submits both to history in general and to one moment of history? Philosophy has not been able to penetrate social reality except by denying its own integrity, as witnessed by the fate of Marxism. But for the pure philosopher the assumption that action is the central reference point for Western culture can only be faint-hearted conformism or a response to metaphysical anxiety. And although Western philosophy has not been a kind of ethereal contemplation, neither is it to be gauged by its effectiveness in making history. It has value only as a spiritual ambition to think the unknowable, and *not* as an ethical system, because it is fundamentally opposed to action, to real life and, ultimately, to common sense.

Without this idealism the whole existence of the West would have been swept away by the most brutal sort of energy. It has been, along with art, literature, and pure science, the great dream of the West, the other dimension of its historical adventure. Such is the paradox of the West, that the most realistic civilization in history has been constantly haunted by the demon of the absolute. This has led to a pervasive ambivalence. The transcendental ego does not place itself at God's service, it measures itself against the world of appearances—not the celestial spheres, but an undifferentiated externality. Science mathematicizes reality, it unifies the fragmentary, idealizes the universe, orders it logically, confers upon it the nobility of thought. But science is also the most realistic of enterprises both in its object and in its results.

Seen from this angle, science gives strong expression to Europe's double face: disorganized idealism and realistic projection, pure intellectuality and forceful action. But as with philosophy, the action we are dealing with here emerges only at the border, where science ends and gives way to technology. The falling away of philosophy into ideology, the devolution of science into technology, that nodal link between two incompatible orders transcends the sphere of culture and reflects the propensities of a civilization that has succeeded—quite

involuntarily—in synthesizing the dual elements of its existence: cultural passion and possessive desire. Should the cultural passion happen to be extinguished, nothing would be left
but the possessive desire, the somber companion of the West,
its torment and its sickness.

## Culture and Modernity

Will European culture become a legacy for others? And who
will these others be? The very notion of a legacy presupposes
the impossibility of reviving any of the high cultures of the past,
but it also implies the existence of a historical intersubjectivity
overshadowing all of them. To put it briefly, culture as the sui
generis organic product of a society tends to be replaced by a
more or less broad cultural consciousness, since modernity has
yet to build its own culture. One wonders if it ever will be able
to, since it lacks the naiveté, the unselfconsciousness, the particularity of closed-off space.

Let us once again address the problem of the genesis of
European culture. At first the European mind revolted against
itself, subjugating, devaluing, or denying its environment
(after borrowing heavily from it). It carried out a huge fictional
return to a single cultural tradition, the Greco-Roman. Self-
destruction, deliverance from the outside world, elimination,
choice: here we have the whole panoply of cultural upheaval.
But in the final analysis the Renaissance is a minor factor, as far
as its achievements go. The sixteenth century failed to push
forward the new culture's lines of force, the conquests of science remained compartmentalized, scholarship persisted in its
quasi-magical framework, the national literatures were barely
formed and still in their infancy. True enough, art was experiencing a splendid flowering, and humanism was pointing the
way to the new culture, but it was the Baroque era that, as far as
science and philosophy are concerned, kept the promises of the
Renaissance, and it did so outside of Italy.

The fading of Italy, the northward migration of cultural creativity, the twisting together of the strands of the Renaissance, humanism, the Reformation and the Counter-Reformation, have evoked different judgments. These phenomena are central to the major historical critique that we find in Hegel, Gramsci, and Weber, and that Trevor-Roper has reworked with considerable acuity. Gramsci isolates the Renaissance as an extraordinary cultural growth, but without broad social foundations, aristocratic by vocation, taking root in Italian cosmopolitanism. He contrasts it with the populism of the Lutheran Reformation, almost echoing Hegel's glorification of the Reformers.

But Protestantism was no more receptive per se than Catholicism to the spirit of inquiry. And the dwindling importance of Italy, as well as the repressive campaign that began there against all forms of innovation arose less out of the internal evolution of Italian society than from the takeover of Catholicism by the Spaniards. Spain's militant Christianity, the fruit of its struggle against Islam, stirred fresh life in reactionary social and mental structures. It imposed on the Counter-Reformation (in itself an effort at purification) a distinctive inquisitorial violence. From then on a pact was sealed uniting Church and State for the purpose of stifling culture, while encouraging intolerance and social conservatism. From then on Italian creativity was condemned by a power foreign to its nature. The fate of Galileo is exemplary in this regard: Galileo, the founder of European science and victim of the Inquisition. Yet it was not Lutheranism that welcomed the new spirit of inquiry, it was the marginal zones of Europe, such as Holland, England, Sweden, and Switzerland.

Owing to its Catholic-Protestant duality and its love of independence, France maintained an ambiguous position. It produced Descartes but sent him into exile. The world of the North was not the creator of European culture, and could not be, but it sheltered and then developed it. Descartes, Bacon, Newton, and Leibniz became possible there. Without the terrible dialectic between the Reformation and the Counter-Reformation they would have been born in Italy. But the essential thing was that the forward thrust went on unbroken, that the migration could occur, thanks to those two motors of Europe's cultural dynamic, mimesis and segmentation. The development of Western *ratio* in the Baroque era was carried out by amateurs, far from the noise of the world, silently, insidiously, with unusual persistency.

But another key factor here was the astonishing solidarity, the binding together, of men of culture from different states and nations. Art, philosophy, and science poured across linguistic frontiers, as civilization united a torn and ravaged Europe. Then the Enlightenment came to extend this effort and bring it to full maturity. Does 1800 mark the end of European culture, properly speaking? Certainly not, but it does signal the end of its formative period, a breakup, the entrance of culture into the field of action, the modification of one by the other and, finally, their going in separate ways. European culture was now solidly established. It would actualize this or that potential feature to a greater or lesser extent, but it would no longer make fundamental innovations. There would be transformations along lines laid out in advance, but no more radically new orientations. This explains the impression of gigantism evoked by the cultural productions of nineteenth-century Europe: people were writing about everything, talking about everything, exploring in all directions. European culture was really becoming aware of itself as the crowning moment of European experience.

There are, of course, two nineteenth centuries, the premodern, preimperialistic phase, lasting roughly till 1860, and the later phase. The first was still deeply rooted in the naive tumult of the eighteenth century, the second was more prosaic but more complete—and, for the world of culture, more tragic. Hegel (like Napoleon and, to a lesser degree, like Goethe) mentally straddled the eighteenth and nineteenth centuries. So did Michelet, whose account of the Revolution came out of his childhood experiences. But the symbolist movement in poetry,

impressionism in painting, the organization of European learning in its supreme institutional embodiment, the German university, even the thought of Karl Marx, already represented
something else: a Europe in revolt against modernity.

It is a gross distortion to define the new territory occupied
by nineteenth-century European culture in terms of a specific
discipline, like a sort of Islamic 'ilm, ignoring the broad areas of
science and sensibility,[9] or the enormous influence of the ideal
of *Wissenschaft*. That would be as false as reducing the varied
intellectual currents of the day to historicism, as widely cultivated as that tendency was.[10] Nineteenth-century European
culture encompassed Lamarck, Ricardo, and Marx as well as
Hugo, Baudelaire, Lessing, Jean-Paul, Manet or Renoir, along
with a host of other names whose very multiplicity implies
development rather than creation. Hegel was one man, but after
him the Hegelians were countless. Rousseau was a solitary, but
French romanticism had a great following.

Development nevertheless implies the death of European
classicism, the means by which European culture had crystallized its first enthusiastic ebullition (art, philosophy, and science) as the discoverer of new principles or even of its own
significance. Then subjectivism in literature and positivism in
science reached their acme, and, indeed, they continue to
amaze us, the former by its depth, the latter by its immense
range. This was the golden age of the novel, of history, and of
inventions. In the novel, society became aware of itself, and the
individual self raised the elements of its sensibility to a highly
complex level. In history the European nations did the same.
They recovered their past, they reread their adventure, and
thought about their origins. The moments when a society is
defining itself, revealing its identity to itself, concluding the job
of building itself and, above all, strongly sensing both the
dynamism of its success and the full extent of the turmoil it has
lived through—these are the times when it stops to reflect upon
the way it came into being.

Politically, the whole nineteenth century could be described as the calm after the storm of the Revolution and the

Empire. Europe set about assimilating, with more or less trouble and not without regrets, the new principles laid down by the Revolution, just when it was becoming politically self-aware, around the time of the Congress of Vienna. This led to a very fine effort to rethink the question of national origins, first of all in France, the homeland of the Revolution. The sequence of the great synthetic historians is a familiar one: Thierry, Quinet, Michelet and, later, Renan and Taine. At the outset personal testimony and enthusiasm were its leading characteristics; later, with Fustel de Coulanges, it was precise erudition. The Germans, too, went from the philosophy of history to the most monumental body of concrete, critical history ever seen.

But then, having established its methodology, history became an anonymous exploration of the human past that did not press into the collective consciousness except when it was explicitly the subject being discussed. The time of the great historians in the French mold had passed. These writers, poets on occasion or full-time (Michelet), discoverers of national roots, memorialists of their age, were all possessed by the same passion for history or for literature and politics.

Voltaire had inaugurated this tradition, Voltaire the militant historian and writer par excellence. Napoleon himself did not simply make history, he pondered it, concerned more with the past than the present, and his judgments turn out to have been invariably correct.[11] A fundamental connection between action, literature, and historical thought remained to testify to the exceptional political adventure that France had gone through and to the tradition laid down by those who had fomented it (Voltaire, Rousseau) or who commented on it (Michelet) or reappropriated and reshaped it as a tool for social control (Guizot, Thiers). With the passage of time this connection narrowed into a simplified blend of literature and politics, owing to the rejection of historical scholarship and the absolute dominance of the philosophical approach.

This impoverishment of the French intellectual scene occurred near the turn of the century, together with the emergence of scientific history and the appearance of the historical specialist cut off from the present. Here we must turn away from France and look to Germany, the birthplace of scholarly historiography, with its profound links to philology. This laborious recovery of all of the human past, this vivid light shed on what time has or has not destroyed, the *correct* method of resurrecting classical antiquity, the ancient East, Islam, the Christian West, and Byzantium—all that unquestionably represents one of the most significant events of the modern era. It revealed a grand universal ambition, transcending the particularism of classical European culture, whose essence we have been trying to discover. Fifty years (1880–1930) were enough to analyze, reconstruct, and explore the density of historical time, as if the learned community of Europe exhausted itself with putting order into the human past, or perhaps because it felt it was the heir and the proud guardian of that past. A critical apparatus had to be built, and a formal methodology. The past had to be stripped of its existential thickness, and this process was extended to the very roots of the West, which were at once exalted and put on trial. From von Ranke, the founding father, to Hefele,[12], Mommsen, Treitschke, Wellhausen, Meyer, and the multitude of their disciples, a sustained effort was made both in analysis and in the publication of major studies.

But the great drama of history is that it remains forever unfinished, whence the feeling of vanity that increases the further one presses one's research. The historian suffocates beneath an accumulated mass of data and details, forever pursuing the absurd hope of one day synthesizing the scattered fragments. But the past is by definition infinite, while the present is limited by its finitude. And history in the past is beset by history in the present, which excludes objectivity, demands meaning, and challenges every cultural consensus, however broad.

Still, the historians' original intention, the passion they displayed, the work they accomplished, were a great achievement that in the future will outlive Europe as one of its essential and most misunderstood enterprises, just as Islamic historiography has survived the disappearance of its original base and has become a crucially important part of the cultural fabric of Islam. Recall the well-known story of the question posed by Tabari to his students: "What if we were to reconstruct the history of humanity ever since Adam?" he asked. "That would consume one lifetime after another," they replied. In Islamic history we find the same gigantism, the same universal aim as in Europe, not to mention a critical methodology.

It is false to confine historical tradition first to the Greek and then to the Western mind. Islamic culture has been, together with Europe, the culture manifesting the strongest sense of the past, made concrete in history on the grand scale, with all the rigor, critical thinking, and cold objectivity which that implies, besides the striking sense of color we find in the first historians, those of the archaic period.[13] In the case of both Europe and Islam we are dealing with two great cultures that constantly refer to history, plunged as deeply as they are into the stream of historical evolution.

What Europe, in its new modern configuration, did in the nineteenth century with history, it had done in the eighteenth century with philosophy, which corresponded more closely to its classical phase. But then science began to reach its apogee, to take on a quasi-definitive shape, to pile up victories. In the eighteenth century its content was still esoteric, fragmentary, and subject to the vagaries of chance. The Committee of Public Safety could cheerfully guillotine Lavoisier without disturbing the rest of Europe, despite his theory of the elements. In the nineteenth century, science organized itself, widened its horizons, all the while remaining faithful to Newton, to the old logical-mathematical foundations, to the notions of law, distance, and force.

Above all it was getting involved with practical applications. But the figure of the scientist-scholar resisted identification with the inventor, that man with only one idea. The savant continued to be guided by the cognitive presupposition, as admirably evidenced by the return to speculative thought around the turn of the century with quantum theory, which was almost contemporaneous with Husserl's return to traditional philosophy, leapfrogging over the nineteenth century and its hunger for concrete results.

But just as phenomenology, which puts up a spirited opposition to scientific objectivism, is a reaction, the last knell of European philosophical classicism, in the same way quantum theory represents a flare-up of lofty scientific aspiration in the classical vein, the ultimate point arrived at by a science that was paradoxically denying its mechanistic basis. For my part, I do not see in this some sort of inexhaustible vitality, but the supreme degree of sophistication on the part of a culture that went through strenuous exertions only to find itself back at square one. When it comes to contemplating the three problems of subjectivity, physical reality, and historical time, the European mind stops short or returns in perplexity to its sources. For a brief moment it goes down into the depths, where it finds only nothingness and uncertainty in the self, the world, and history.[14]

In fact, a strident, unmistakable, basic contradiction exists between the speculative order and the domain of action, between Western culture and modernity. Modernity is becoming universal, while Western culture, *in the West*, continues to follow its own particularist line in, among other things, high speculative science. This contradiction did not appear just yesterday. In 1800 there was a brilliant civilization in Europe, as there was till not so long ago, and a brilliant culture within the framework of a normal historical development. Napoleon lived and moved in a world not radically different from that of Mahmud of Ghazna. At least at the beginning of his career Napoleon sensed how feeble Europe's impact was on the history of the planet. He was fascinated by the gigantic scale of Asia, the womb of nations and empires. He thought in terms of peoples and territories, in the context of an agrarian, mercantile, and manufacturing economy.

He took scientists with him to Egypt and thereby gained an awareness of the importance of science as Europe's distinctive glory. Yet his chemists had done little more than run experiments with retorts, like master-magicians.[15] Sixty years later

Napoleon III threw the age-old map of the East into confusion by digging the Suez Canal. Between the rule of uncle and nephew the age of capitalist, mechanized modernity had arrived, the reign of European man over nature had begun.[16] Spengler's antimodernism leads him to date the end of European culture at about 1800, thereupon substituting for the culture the notion of civilization, which is synonymous with decline. One need not accept his guiding assumption, which ultimately amounts to a visceral critique of modernity, of the sort the nineteenth century produced in such abundance.

But it is important to focus on the concept of modernity as a break in the specific historical evolution of Europe as well as in the normal course of human history, whose unity, *pace* Spengler, must be rethought. We cannot deny that in its origins modernity was to some extent nourished by the intellectual soil of the complex known as Europe. But that civilization responded to modernity as to a foreign body issuing from within itself, or as to a force whose appearance could be interpreted equally well as contingent or necessary. Modernity was a silent, autonomous structure, "which at bottom had as much difficulty conquering geographical Europe as it did the rest of the world,"[17] since it took more than a hundred and fifty years to penetrate the most refractory layers even of the European world. With its variants (the diverse forms of socialism or capitalism) it now imposes itself on the entire planet as a model whose core is industry, technology, and industrialized labor. It has co-opted science as its instrument, and so it presupposes a certain amount of scientific development, but not the necessity of reproducing the whole trajectory followed by European science nor the need to attain its highest cognitive levels. This is amply proved by the example of America's last 100 years and by the obvious and lasting advantages that commerce has over learning. And we are familiar with the global implications of this: colonialism, imperialism, revolutions, headlong economic development, and the unification of the world.

The historical problem here is a many-faceted one. We have already mentioned the issue raised by the temporal discontinuity that confers an extravagantly privileged on the status of the contemporary era.[18] Then there is the extreme difficulty of trying to separate modernity, as an objective structure, from the mass of specifically Western values that have become associated with it by a sort of historical accident. A final problem is that the status of Western culture within the new, broader version of modernity remains to be defined. Does the West propose to construct the culture of modernity all by itself, or is its own culture destined to perish, like all the others?

Our nightmares are now knocking on the door. Modernity deified is man devalued, history discredited, and humanity divided into two polar opposites, modern and traditional. If modernity is removed from its Western substrate, it cannot be implanted elsewhere except through the mediation of ideology; in other words, by the negation of a culture's essence. If this removal does not occur, then we still have cultural alienation. Finally, if Western culture has had its lease on life renewed for a century, it is because it has escaped contamination by a system that permeates everywhere, but slowly. So it has developed its possibilities to the ultimate limit, but, like civilization, it comes to an end once modernity sets about constructing its own peculiar civilization and culture.

For our purposes, this is where a new series of questions comes up, questions which Islam asks of the West, and the West of Islam.

# 8

# By Way of Conclusion: Islam, the West, and Modernity

The problem of the cultural Westernization of the Muslim world, a much broader issue than mere alienation on the part of the colonizing power, was raised at the beginning of the century by Orientalists, statesmen, and "Muslim" thinkers, by men like Becker or Atatürk or Taqizadeh. Present-day circumstances have both left this problem behind and posed it anew. On the one hand, the rejection of colonialist domination and the partial but important liberation movements that followed had the effect of reintegrating the Muslim countries into the stream of contemporary history. On the other hand, the temptation of technological modernization has never presented itself more insistently than it does today, as if rediscovered historical dignity demanded imitation of the victorious-vanquished West. Muslims are no longer being asked to Westernize their souls to find their place in the world, but to rationalize and modernize their lives.

The old conflicts between Islam and the West are now especially outdated because a unified Islam has ceased to exist, while the West is perceived and by this time perceives itself as a heterogeneous composite, and today's modernity has a different meaning from yesterday's. So long as the West exercised its dominance directly, it assumed that, since Islam was outside history, it was all of a piece. Similarly, the West once managed

to synthesize its religion, its culture, its civilization, its technological modernity—something it neither does, nor can do, any
longer. Nietzsche had already fulminated against modernity
and, after him, Spengler distinguished the concept of Western
culture from that of civilization (imperialism, industrialism—in
a word, modernity).

Now we find that Western culture in its various aspects has
been radically fragmented, authentic Western civilizations are
coming apart, and the monster devouring them can produce
nothing but a subculture and a subcivilization.

Western *culture* was bound up with moral values as much as
with a certain fundamental aspiration. Both of these, however,
have managed to change their content while protecting their
overall purpose. The *civilization* of the West was its way of
envisaging life as a whole, its attempt to conquer nature, its
endeavor to build, in the cities and the countryside, a particular
human existence, and to provide an orientation for human
activity. Up until the Industrial Revolution there was a culture
and a civilization, and nothing more. Later, and until recently,
these two structures succeeded in dominating the nascent
power of technology, civilization by harnessing it, culture by
simply ignoring it.

But the invasion of technological modernity has broken the
rhythms of the one and drained the substance of the other. The
malaise of the West arises from the fact that it can save neither
its culture nor its civilization, because modernity has imposed
its own patterns, which operate by modernist logic. If the West
desired to move boldly and bring about this sort of separation, it
would not be able to, precisely because of the long and deep
influence that industrialization has had on civilization, as well
as because, more significantly, technological thinking itself
derives, even though indirectly, from a fundamental cultural
choice in favor of rationality. The renewed stress on regional-
ism, the impassioned questions raised about the anguish of
modern times, the proliferation of sects, the culture of marginality, the rediscovery of communitarian values—all these
reactions testify confusedly to the same malaise over the rising

tide of inhumanity. And this response comes just when every-where else one sees at once the longing for that modernity and the extreme difficulty of getting it.

The new voices (still only a minority) now heard in the West entreating Muslims to remain themselves represent, first of all, the naive unhappy consciousness of the West which, confront-ing its own painful alienation, sees in a mythical (or real) vision of Islam the obverse of its sufferings: a sense of happiness, of spirituality, of community. But a more rational consciousness goes further and warns against unchecked development and cultural Westernism. The Muslim world, it says, is going through a pseudomorphosis comparable to that of the Hellenis-tic Orient. Napoleon, the man of the West, is the modern ver-sion of Alexander, the man of Hellenism. If modern intellectuals help to drive Islam into a state of alienation, no doubt within two or three generations we shall see Islam recaptured by the most profound forces within it.[1] But to argue this way pre-supposes that Islam has a special capacity for renewal as well as a single, uniform destiny, two points that remain to be proved. And to speak of pseudomorphosis is to call for a "revolution in the East," led not by Islam but more likely by a form of Marxism playing the role of primitive Islam.

A more coherent attitude is found on the part of Western thinkers who have launched a counterassault on modernity by appealing to Western "tradition," and beyond that to every kind of spiritual, nonrational, or antihistorical approach.[2] This is a matter of challenging not just technological modernity but the whole intellectual sequence that produced it, whether in the West or outside the West (and at an earlier date): Aristotle, Averroes, Scholasticism, the Renaissance, the whole rationalist current in science and history. Plato will be invoked against Aristotle, Avicenna against Averroes, Paracelsus against Des-cartes, Nietzsche or Spengler against Hegel. Appeals to myth, symbolism, and the tradition of spiritual Muslims will serve to denounce the mutilation of *episteme* by scientism, rationalism, and historicism.

These three challenges—ethical, historical, and anthropological in the broad sense—deserve the closest attention. They constitute a new departure in the West, even where the principal line of criticism of "technological civilization" hardly ventures beyond the Western horizon, ignores other cultures and, until now, has displayed little concern with underlying historical factors or with the task of reconciling social criticism, criticism of civilization, and pure intellectual research. In the Muslim countries or, more generally speaking, the nonindustrialized world, these challenges ought to give food for thought to all those now fascinated by a skimpy, narrow rationalism.

But despite their intention of bringing the great non-Western cultures into their notion of humanity, these dissenting voices (still widely scattered and confused), by the very fact that they come from the West, may be expressing no more than another phase in the crisis of Western consciousness. They cannot become universal and so acquire real validity except insofar as a new historical equilibrium puts the West and the rest of the world on a footing of equality. The truth is, they seem to ignore real history, its struggles, its violence, and its demands.

Because the West is there, with its power and technology. It has dominated and still dominates the picture. And so long as *Homo occidentalis* continues to act out his Promethean vision, he forces his rhythm and his choices on others, under pain of subjection or historical death. The West has not only goaded the world into fighting against it with its own weapons, it exports and imposes the frenzy for development on which it itself is now choking.

So we must at all costs maintain both a sense of rationality and a sense of history. On this point, Laroui's observations are correct: however false it may be in absolute terms, the notion of "backwardness," as applied to the Muslim world, is nonetheless real. But what does it actually mean? It means that one fine day the West broke away from the pack of its fellows, running ahead, exhausting both itself and them. But in this unsporting race, with its peculiar rules, the one who jumps out ahead stifles his adversary, and those who fall behind are crushed. Their backwardness is the dark side of the breathless race run by the West, which has chosen the pace, the terrain, and the goal.

Because this "backwardness" does exist, and because modernity includes important benefits, along with alienation, it is necessary to go on trying to catch up. But because this gap cannot possibly be made up, it is crucial to preserve other forms of value: an identity, a culture, a civilization. Islam will not be able to match the West's technological capacity, its science, or its power. That is not to say that it should drop out of the race, but rather that it should not get lost in the confusion. In a word, it should safeguard, cultivate, and refine its share, which is great, in the human enterprise.

The inner suffering of the West comes from the fact that its culture has been devoured by modernity. But it is true that India suffers from hunger, not from a lack of spirituality, nor from an excess of that spirituality. For the first time in history a kind of local modernity is becoming universal, attaching itself to a whole spectrum of cultures. These cultures have received it from outside, as a gift once beneficial and poisonous (and in any case heavy with fate), and so they remain less contaminated than the West, but they are just as threatened by it, though for different reasons. The eclipse they have undergone, however, represents one of the hazards of life.

In the West, in a world where God has been expelled, the conflict between culture and modernity has brought alienation. Japan, which long tried to preserve the most intimate part of its being, is now witnessing the spectacle of its devastated culture. More than ever, people speak of confrontation between civilizations, but in reality civilizations clash only when heterogeneous racial groups coexist in a given society. As far as historical violence goes, only powers conflict and only for the sake of power: the murderous history of a Europe united by civilization stands as evidence for that.

So the dialectic of power will continue, somewhere or other, openly or in disguise. Yet in the sphere we are dealing with the pattern emerging is not a confrontation between civilizations but of each one with modernity. And if there is any sort of solidarity that can provide a basis for a truly universal aspiration, it is surely the solidarity of cultures, including that of the West, against the enemy that denies them all: uncontrolled modernity. Within this framework Islam can send home its sublime message.

# Notes

*Introduction*

1. Lévi-Strauss, *Anthropologie Structurale*, II (Paris: Plon, 1973), p. 365 f.

## 1: From the Medieval Vision to Modern Visions

1. Claude Cahen, "L'Accueil des chrétiens d'Orient à l'Islam," *Revue de l'histoire des religions*, I (1964).

2. The arguments presented by A. Abel in *Studia Islamica* (1963) are convincing.

3. L. Gardet and Anawati, *Introduction à la théologie musulmane* (Paris: Vrin, 1948).

4. Marc Bloch, *La Societé feodale* (Paris: Albin-Michel) I:13.

5. R. W. Southern, *Western Views of Islam in the Middle Ages* (Cambridge, Mass.: Harvard University Press, 1962), p. 19.

6. Norman Daniel, *Islam and the West: The Making of an Image* (Edinburgh, 1960), p. 6.

7. Orientalism came directly from this source, and it continues the medieval polemic.

8. Daniel, *Islam and the West*, p. 146.

9. Ibid., p. 143.

10. One can find the same idea in Lévi-Strauss, *Tristes Tropiques*.

11. Daniel, *Islam and the West*, p. 109.

12. Pascal, *Pensées*, La Pléiade edition, pt. 2, sec. 1, par. 402.

13. M. Rodinson, *The Legacy of Islam* (Oxford: Oxford University Press, 1975). See also Daniel, *Islam, Europe and Empire* (Edinburgh, 1966), a fundamental work for the whole modern era.

## 2: French Intellectuals and Islam

1. Norman Daniel, *Islam and the West*, pp. 290—291.

2. Napoleon said that, "Here Voltaire had done a disservice to history and to the human heart." See Norman Daniel, *Islam, Europe and Empire*, p. 29.

3. It should be noted that in the eighteenth century there were many broad exceptions to this pattern, especially de Boulainvilliers in his *Vie de Mahomet* (Amsterdam: Francois Changuion, 1731). For many Enlightenment writers Muhammad took on the features of a wise reformer.

4. Edward Gibbon, *Decline and Fall of the Roman Empire* (Bury, 1900—1914), chap. 50.

5. Voltaire liked to keep informed about Ottoman affairs. He read the work by Cantemir with interest and reacted to it.

6. Voltaire, quoted by Brunschvig, *Classicisme et declin culturel dans l'histoire de l'Islam* (Paris: Maisonneuve, 1956), p. 31.

7. Volney, *Les Ruines*, in *Oeuvres complètes* (Paris, 1860), p. 65.

8. Ibid., p. 42.

9. Ibid., p. 43.

10. Volney, *Travels in Egypt and Syria*, in *Oeuvres complètes*, pp. 288—289.

11. Volney, *Voyage en Syrie et en Egypte pendant les années 1783—1785* (Paris, 1787), pp. 301—310.

12. Chateaubriand's voyage was also a mystical and archaeological journey to the sources of Greek antiquity. His interest in Islam could only be secondary. Ultimately Islam remained for him a state of barbarism organized and humanized by religion, the universal human language.

13. Moënis Taha-Hussein, *Presence de l'Islam dans la litterature romantique en France*, p. 144; Lamartine, *Voyage en Orient* (Paris: Hachette, 1875).

14. Taha-Hussein, *Presence de l'Islam*, p. 160.

15. Messiaen, *Gerard de Nerval*, Paris, 1945; J. de Corti, 1968), p. 5.

16. Albert Béguin, *Gerard de Nerval*, p. 64.

17. Louis Massignon, *Opera minora* (Paris: Presses Universitaires de France, 1963) 2:162.

18. See the example of Gustave Lebon, *La Civilisation des Arabes* (Paris, 1884).

19. Henri Bergson, *The Two Sources of Morality and Religion*. Yet by far the most important continuator of Bergson is a Muslim, Muhammad Iqbal, though he does come from India.

20. Germany, the spectator of a history being made elsewhere, compensated for that through ideology. This is Althusser's idea, which I wholly subscribe to.

21. Jean-Paul Sartre, *Critique de la raison dialectique* (Paris: Galli-mard, 1960), p. 190: "To treat a man like a dog, one must first have recognized him as a man." See also pp. 670—679. Sartre often refers to Algeria as a typical case of bourgeois colonial exploitation.

## 3. European Scholarship and Islam

1. Ernest Renan, "Islam and Science," in *Oeuvres complètes* (Paris: Calmann-Lévy, 1947) 1:945—965.

2. Ibid., 3:20—365.

3. Renan, *The Future of Science* in ibid., 3:877, for example.

4. Renan (Paris: Calmann-Lévy, n.d.).

5. Renan, *Memories of Childhood and Youth*, in *Oeuvres complètes* I:126—137.

6. Ibid., 1:134.

7. Ibid., 3:85.

8. Renan was quick to notice the hedonistic life of the philos-ophers. On Avicenna, see Ibn Khallikan, *Wafayat*, which stresses his amazing sensuality.

9. Renan, "L'Islamisme et la science," *Oeuvres complètes* 1:955. This idea was probably borrowed from Voltaire's *Essai sur les moeurs*.

10. al-Afghani responded to Renan's lecture on Islam and science in a piece (written in excellent French) in the *Moniteur*. A. Hourani quotes a passage from it in *Arabic Thought in the Liberal Age* (Oxford: Oxford University Press, 1962) that a modern scholar would not dis-own, whereas Renan's ideas are pathetically outdated.

11. I shall pass over its oft-denounced racist quality.

12. Joseph Needham makes a similar suggestion in *Science and Civilization in China*, 5 vols. (New York: Cambridge University Press, 1954—1970). Later on I shall return to the devastating effect of the Counter-Reformation.

13. On the subject of the *obshchina*, Marx felt the temptation of a world that was archaic, spontaneous, stable, and solid. See J. J. Lenz, *De l'Amérique et de la Russie* (Paris: Édition du Seuil, 1972), p. 218.

14. Hichem Djaït, *La Personnalité et le devenir arabo-islamiques* (Paris: Édition du Seuil, 1974).

15. Quoted by Waardenburg, *L'Islam dans le miroir de l'Occident* (Paris-The Hague: Mouton, 1963), p. 196.

16. MacDonald and Von Grunebaum, *L'Islam Medieval* (Paris: Payot, 1962), p. 252.

17. Abel and Bousquet, in Brunschvig, *Classicisme et déclin culturel dans l'histoire de l'Islam* (Paris: Maisonneuve, 1956).

18. Reinhart Dozy, *Histoire des musulmans d'Espagne* (Leyden, 1932) 1:63—68.

19. Ibid., p. 67.

20. Wellhausen, *Das Arabische Reich und sein Sturz*, Arabic trans. (Cairo, 1958), p. 155.

21. Especially the American school, which accentuates political science. And popular Western thinking is more hostile to the Arabs than to Islam, insofar as it manages to separate the two.

22. Perosphile esotericism shares this vision.

23. Goldziher, *Mohammedanische Studien* (Halle, 1890) 1:101—107.

24. Goldziher, *Le Dogme et la loi d'Islam*, p. 23; Waardenburg, *L'Islam dans le miroir de l'Occident*, p. 44.

25. Snouck-Hurgronje cited in Waardenburg, *L'Islam dans le miroir de l'Occident*, p. 41.

26. Becker in Waardenburg, *L'Islam dans le miroir de l'Occident*, p. 131.

27. Becker, *Islamstudien* (Leipzig) 1:405.

28. A. Musil, *Manners and Customs of the Rwala Beduins* (1928); Ed. Doutte, *Magie et Religion dans l'Afrique du Nord* (1909). See also the work of Westermarck and, more recently, Berque and G. Tillon. Berque tries to get beyond colonialistic ethnology, and largely succeeds.

29. With some exceptions, the most notable being Robertson Smith (whom Freud knew well), the author of *Kinship and Marriage in Early Arabia* (1907), an essay in historical ethnology. We should also note the emergence of an American school of Islamic ethnology, with Gellner and Geertz.

30. Fanon, *Les Damnes de la terre* (Paris: Maspero, 1961), pp. 224—235.

31. Lévi-Strauss, *Tristes Tropiques*, trans., John and Doreen Weightman (New York: Atheneum, 1975), pp. 394—410.

32. Ibid., p. 400.

33. Ibid., p. 401.

34. Ibid., p. 404.

35. Ibid., p. 408.

36. Ibn Sa'd, *Tabaqat*, vol. 3, and passim.

37. Islamic society unquestionably does manifest a certain particularism, which Lévi-Strauss has more or less grasped.

38. And it is in this sense that G. von Grunebaum's argument on the absence of humanism in Islam has to be corrected. See *Islam mediéval* (Paris: Payot, 1962), p. 253.

39. E. Sivan, *L'Islam et la croisade, idéologie et propagande dans les réactions musulmanes aux croisades* (Paris, 1968).

40. And of all the traditional Oriental civilizations. In this context one might go back to Hegel's case against Hinduism and relate to Islam what he says about Christianity: "This is the grand distinction, that

here Religion holds the same position towards *all*; that, although the son of a worker becomes a worker, the son of a peasant a peasant . . . the *religious element* stands in the same relation to all, and all are invested with an absolute value by religion. In India the direct contrary is the case. In this respect [in the Christian West] the higher classes are equal to the lower; and while religion is the higher sphere in which all sun themselves, equality before the law—rights of person and of property—are gained for every class. [In India] humanity generally, human duty and human feeling do not manifest themselves; we find only duties assigned to the several castes. . . . Morality and human dignity are unknown; evil passions have their full swing; the Spirit wanders into the Dream-World, and the highest state is Annihilation." *Lectures on the Philosophy of History*, trans. J. Sibree (London: Henry G. Bohn, 1857), pp. 154–155 (slightly altered). What Hegel says about Christianity is even more applicable to Islam. In morality and law, Islam gave the East a principle of universality and humanization. It crossed the threshold effectively separating two types of human beings. It transcends the absurdity found in the customs, legal systems, ethics, and religions of the Orient.

## 4. Islam and German Thought

1. This analysis omits contemporary Germany, which has nothing to offer of historical interest on this topic.

2. Renan, "Averroès et l'averroïsme," in *Oeuvres complètes* 3:225.

3. And in the United States, but only late in the day.

4. Bismarck regarded Islam with contempt.

5. Rashid Ridha, *Tarikh Muhammad 'Abduh* 1:921. This viewpoint has to be corrected by the observation that the French monarchy and its two Empires were much less harsh than the radical Republic.

6. But even at the core of the Neo-Destour there was some positive feeling toward the Axis.

7. Lévi-Strauss, *Tristes Tropiques*, p. 403.

8. *Shawqiyyat* 2:5 (Shakespeare), but Shawqi also admired the creative genius of France.

9. Hegel, *Lectures on the Philosophy of History*, p. 115.

10. I.e., Islam and not simply the teaching of Muhammad.

11. Hegel, *Lectures*, p. 370.

12. Ibid.

13. Ibid., p. 372.

14. Was it Hegelianism that caused Gramsci to devalue the Renaissance and concentrate on the Reformation? See Gramsci's *Prison Notebooks*.

15. Oswald Spengler, *Decline of the West*. One-volume edition, translated by Charles Francis Atkinson (New York: Knopf, 1939).

16. Muhammad Iqbal, *Reconstruire la pensée religieuse de l'Islam* (Paris: Maisonneuve, 1955), p. 154; Bultmann, *History and Eschatology;* Wittfogel, *Le Despotisme oriental* (Paris: Éditions de Minuit, 1964).

17. Spengler, *Decline* 1:248. Hegel remarks that the internal form of the *Thousand and One Nights* is ancient Egyptian. A number of German Orientalists, of whom the best known is G. von Grunebaum, have drawn attention to the way the *Nights* borrowed from Greek tradition, in *Islam medieval* (pp. 321–347). This points up the lasting, if not obvious, imprint of Hellenism on the East, but the essence of the *Thousand and One Nights* strikes me as thoroughly Oriental and Arab-Persian.

18. Spengler, *Decline* 1:183.

19. This point of view is clearly the opposite of Renan's.

20. Spengler, *Decline* 1:213.

21. Ibid., 2:260.

22. Ibid., 2:304.

23. All philosophies of history tend to think that when a civilization succeeds it is already in decline.

24. Muhammad Iqbal, *Reconstruire la pensée religieuse de l'Islam,* p. 155.

25. Godelier, *Sur les sociétés précapitalistes* (Paris: Éditions Sociales, 1970).

## 5. The Historical Dynamic

1. It seems that old Kant foresaw that European technology would end by swamping all the continents, but he was more reticent about the spread of humanism. See Hannah Arendt, *Vies Politiques* (Paris: Gallimard, 1974).

2. Maurice Lombard, *Espaces et réseaux du haut moyen âge* (Paris-The Hague: Mouton, 1972).

3. G. Hourani, *Arab Seafaring in the Indian Ocean* (1951); Sauvaget, *Relation de la Chine et de l'Inde* (Paris: Les Belles Lettres, 1948).

4. George Steiner, *La Culture contre l'homme* (Paris: Édition du Seuil, 1971).

5. Marshall G. Hodgson, *The Venture of Islam,* 3 vols., *Conscience and History in World Civilization* (Chicago: University of Chicago Press, 1975), 2:332.

6. Ibid.

## 6. Islam: Civilization, Culture, Politics

1. Goldziher, *Le Dogme et la loi de l'Islam* (Paris: Éditions P. Geuthner, 1920), p. 23.

2. Waardenburg, *L'Islam dans le miroir de l'occident,* p. 41.

3. Gellner, repeated by Laroui in *Histoire du Maghreb* (Paris: Maspero, 1971).

4. D. Cantemir, *The History of the Ottoman Empire* (Bucharest, 1971).

5. On this subject, see my earlier work, *La Personnalité et le devenir arabo-islamiques* (Paris: Édition du Seuil, 1974).

## 7. Europe as a Particular Case

1. Taine, *Origines de la France contemporaine* (Paris: Robert Laffont, 1971), pp. 115—129.

2. Michelet, *Histoire de la Révolution française* (Paris: Robert Laffont, 1971).

3. Papadopoulos insists far too strongly on this idea. See especially his article in *Annales* 3 (1973), "Esthetique de l'art musulman. La peinture." Need we recall that the mystical intention in art, if it exists, is always blended together confusedly with the aesthetic intention? The fact remains that the passion for painting has been repressed in Islamic civilization: miniaturization is no doubt a defensive reaction to this, as is unrealism. Such as it is, this sort of painting seems more refined than the Western variety. And it is certain that it has a genuinely Islamic character, despite the Chinese influences (which have been greatly exaggerated).

4. There is a serious correction of Newtonian mechanics in the *First Metaphysical Principles of the Science of Nature* and the *Critique of Judgment*. On this point, see Roger Ayrault, *La Genese du romantisme allemand* (Paris: Aubier, 1961), pp. 254—274.

5. Plato showed the way, but the concentration on the ego is authentically European, as Spengler realized. Kojève, too, shows, in the matter of dialectic, the profound difference between Plato and Hegel. See *Introduction à la lecture de Hegel* (Paris: Gallimard, 1947), pp. 455—458.

6. Granet in his preface to the translation of Husserl's *Krisis*.

7. Merleau-Ponty, *Le Visible et l'invisible* (Paris: Gallimar, 1964).

8. Although the Scot David Hume was a founding figure.

9. Foucault, *Les Mots et les choses* (Paris: Gallimard, 1966).

10. Laroui, *La Crise des intellectuels arabes* (Paris: Maspero, 1974).

11. In Napoleon's eyes, the Greeks did not win the battle of Marathon, which had neither victors nor vanquished, and was of secondary importance to the Persian Empire. He thought that the Arabs conquered the world so quickly because they had gained experience in the wars of the Arabian Peninsula (the *ridda*), etc. See the *Mémorial de Sainte-Hélène* (Paris, 1823).

12. Special attention should be given to the trends in Christian exegesis, particularly to the Tübingen and Mainz schools, which

culminated in the work of Adolf Harnack. David Strauss was primarily a post-Hegelian philosopher, but Renan borrowed heavily from him. The 1880s mark the surrender of French scholarship to German scholarship and the glorification in Germany itself of German culture, in the sense of *Wissenschaft*, not as linguistic and literary perfection, an honor that was always reserved for the genius of France. Taine has some fine pages (in his *Origines*) attacking the incapacity of French culture to integrate the learned disciplines, and for its mania for formalism and generalizations.

13. Abu Mikhnaf, Sayf, al-Haytham b. Adi, Mada'ini. In its beginnings Islamic historiography was purely Arab and almost contemporary with the events it recorded. "All history is contemporary history," said Croce. He should have specified, all history caught up in its own world, but not the proudly contemplative effort to resurrect the most distant past in its entirety.

14. Hans Reichenbach, *Philosophic Foundations of Quantum Mechanics* (University of California Press, 1946). Unlike the theory of relativity, quantum theory is not based on a single clear principle, but it goes further in its revision of the foundations of classical physics, since it questions the principle of causality. Its development comes in three stages: (1) 1900—1925, with Planck, Einstein, Bohr; (2) 1925—1930, with de Broglie, Schrödinger (who discovered the two fundamental differential equations), Max Born, Heisenberg, Dirac, and (3) 1930—1940, with the same protagonists, especially Schrödinger.

15. Their brief presence in the East nevertheless left some traces, but that is another problem. On the subject of their influence on Tahtawi, by way of his master, see A. Hourani, *Arabic Thought in the Liberal Age*.

16. Along with the reign over his fellow man, whose methodical exploitation he organized. The roots of capitalism go far back—perhaps to the Middle Ages—and have to be related to the other elements in the evolution of Western history. But it sprouted in darkness, with apparent autonomy, and it paralleled other evolutionary developments. The link joining science, democracy, and capitalism acquires its necessary character only through an a posteriori reconstruction. In itself, it is contingent, except perhaps during its underground formative period.

17. Laroui, "Europe et non-Europe," in *La Crise des intellectuels arabes*, except that he is speaking not of the concept of Europe but of modernity as a purely economic-technological formation.

18. This is Raymond Aron's point of view in his introduction to a work by many hands, entitled *L'Historien face à l'ethnologue et au politicologue*. According to this position, the past could never explain or help foresee the future. Historicism and Marxism are both dismissed, even though historicism postulates that the present is destined to become part of the past and can claim something of a privileged status only as present. See Althusser, *Pour Marx* (Paris: Maspero, 1971).

## 8. By Way of Conclusion

1. This is the opinion expressed by Richard Bulliet, of Columbia University, in a discussion published in *Diogène* (1976), n. 95.

2. This is the viewpoint of esoteric scholars such as de Corbin, for example, in his *Islam iranien*, or of G. Durand in a rich, stirring, but debatable book, *Science de l'homme et tradition* (Paris, 1975).

# Glossary of Proper Names and Arabic Terms

Prepared by Edmund Burke III
University of California, Santa Cruz

Abbasid: Islamic dynasty that ruled A.D. 750—1250. From their capital in Baghdad, the Abbasid caliphs ruled an empire which, at its height, stretched from northwest India to northwest Africa.

Abduh, Shaykh Muhammad: Egyptian Islamic modernist scholar and religious leader (1849—1905), co-editor (with Jamal al-Din al-Afghani) of *al-Urwa al-Wuthqa*, a short-lived but important journal of the pre-1914 Islamic revival.

Abdul Hamid II: Ruler of the Ottoman empire (1876—1909), known for his restrictive policies on intellectuals and minorities.

Abu-al-Ala al-Maari: See al-Maari, Abu-al-Ala.

Abu Mikhnaf: Abu Mikhnaf Lut ibn Yahya (d. 774) wrote numerous accounts of the exploits of pre-Islamic Arabian tribes.

Abu Qurra: Theodorus Abu Qurra, Christian author of the theological treatise *De Cultu Imaginum* (c. 877), one of the oldest Arabic paper manuscripts.

al-Afghani, Jamal al-Din: A prominent exponent of Muslim unity (1838–1897), and co-editor (with Muhammad Abduh) of the influential newspaper, *al-Urwa al-Wuthqa*. Also known as al-Asadabadi.

Asharism: School of thought of Abu al-Hasan al-Ash'ari (d. 935) which sought to develop a defense of Islamic doctrines via the application of the principles of *kalam*, or systematic theological disputation.

Atatürk: Honorific name of Mustafa Kemal (1881–1938), Ottoman military leader, later first president of the Republic of Turkey. Under his rule Turkey became a secular democracy linked to the West.

Averroes: Latin name for Ibn Rushd (1126–1198), an Andalusian qadi and physician, known in the West chiefly as an important Aristotelian thinker.

Avicenna: Latin name for Abu Ali Ibn Sina (980–1037), a Central Asian philosopher and physician, known primarily for application of Aristotelian thought to Islamic religious thought.

Ba'ath party. See Baathist.

Baathist: A follower of the Socialist Arab Ba'ath party, established in 1947 in Syria; currently Syria and Iraq have Ba'athist governments.

Bash Hamba, Ali: Tunisian nationalist and journalist (d. 1918), a leader of the Young Tunisian movement, and editor of *Le Tunisien*.

Basra: City in southeastern Iraq.

al-Biruni, Abu al-Rayhan: Islamic mathematician, astronomer, and philosopher (973–1050) from Khwarazm, in central Asia.

Bourguiba: Habib ibn Ali Bourguiba (1903–    ) first president of Tunisia, and founder of the nationalist Neo-Destour Party, which gained independence from France in 1956.

Dar al-Harb: "The abode of war": in the classical Islamic distinction, that portion of the world not under Muslim rule, as contrasted to the portion under Muslim rule, "Dar al-Islam" (q.v.).

Dar al-Islam: "The abode of Islam": in the classical Islamic distinction, that portion of the world under Islamic rule as contrasted to the portion not ruled by Muslims, the "Dar al-Harb" (q.v.).

din: (Arabic) religion.

falsafa: Islamic philosophy, especially that influenced by Hellenistic moral and natural philosophy.

Farghana: A city in Central Asia, in the Tarim basin.

Fatamid: An Islamic dynasty of seven-imam Shi'ites (969–1171) which at its height ruled an empire centered in Egypt that extended from eastern Algeria to Arabia.

fiqh: Islamic jurisprudence; the discipline of explaining the .ul shariah (q.v.); also the resultant body of rules.

Fuqaha: Arabic (sing. faqih); exponents of fiqh (q.v.).

Gokalp, Ziya: Late nineteenth-century Turkish nationalist writer and ideologue; his ideas were taken up in the Turkish Republic.

hadith: Report of sayings and doings of the Prophet, or such reports collectively. Six such collections are recognized by Sunnis, four by Shi'ites. Sometimes translated as "tradition."

hajj: The annual Pilgrimage to Mecca in the month of Dhu al-Hijja, the last month of the Muslim year, an obligation incumbent on every adult Muslim, at least once in a lifetime. Also, an honorific title given to one who has made the pilgrimage.

hallajism: Followers of the Sufi mystic and poet Mansur al-Hallaj (d. 922), executed for heresy; also the high love mysticism associated with him.

Hamidian Empire: See Abdul Hamid II.

hammam: Muslim bathhouse.

Harra: Battle (c. 683) at which the Medinese were defeated by the Umayyads, led by Muslim b. 'Uqba al-Murri (q.v.).

al-Haytham b. Adi, Abu Abd al-Rahman: Abbasid court historian and traditionist (738–822).

Hijra: The flight of Muhammad and his followers from Mecca to Medina; the year it occurred, 622, is the base-year of the Islamic calendar.

Husayn: Last male descendant of Muhammad; he died in battle against Yazid I.

Husayni, Hajj Amin al-: The Chief Mufti of Jerusalem under the Palestine Mandate (1922–1948), a leader of the Palestinian national movement.

Ibn al-Zubayr, Abdullah: Claimant to the title of caliph (681–692) and leader of Meccan faction in the period of the second fitnah, or civil war.

Ibn Batuta, Muhammad ibn Abdullah: A native of Tangier, Morocco, and famous world traveler (1304–1377). A contemporary of Marco Polo, ibn Batuta visited Africa, India, China, and the Middle East and later wrote an extensive account of his travels.

Ibn Fadlan: Ahmad ibn Fadlan ibn-Hammad, Muslim traveler whose account of his trip (921) to the kingdom of the Bulghars is one of the earliest reliable accounts of southern Russia.

Ibn Khaldun, Abd al-Rahman: Islamic philosopher and historian of Tunisian origin (1332–1406), best known for his *Muqaddimah*, a three-volume introduction to history.

Ibrahim Pasha: The son and successor of Muhammad Ali Pasha (d. 1848), ruler of Egypt, especially known as military commander and administrator.

Idrisi, Muhammad al-Sharif: Muslim geographer (d. 1169), author of *The Book of Roger* written for Roger II, Norman ruler of Sicily.

Iqbal, Muhammad: Indian Muslim poet and philosopher (1876–1938).

Ishraqi: A school of Neo-Platonic Sufi philosophy most identified with Ibn Arabi (d. 1240) and Yahya Suhravardi (d. 1191).

jahiliyya: The time of ignorance; for Muslims, the period which predated the coming of Islam to Arabia.

Jaxartes: The Syr Darya, a central Asian river.

al-Jaylani, Rashid Ali: Iraqi military officer and prime minister (1940–1941) who sought an alliance with Germany. (Also al-Gailani.)

jihad: Struggle; holy war. A basic Islamic concept, it refers to the moral struggle of individuals to master their own passions, and to the struggle for justice in the community which is Islam; by extension, to defend Dar al-Islam (q.v.) against its enemies.

Kairouan: City in south-central Tunisia, established by the Arab conquerors c. 670.

kalam: Discussion, on the basis of Muslim assumptions, of questions of theology and cosmology; sometimes called "scholastic theology."

Kavadh: Sasanid Persian emperor, ruled 488–496 and 499–531.

Khurasan: Province of northeastern Iran, in Abbasid times an important military and cultural center.

Kufa: City in central Iraq, founded c. 638 by early Arab conquerors.

al-Maari, Abu-al-Ala (973–1058): A major Abbasid poet and letter-writer, known best for his *Luzumiyyat*.

Mada'ini: Abbasid historian and traditionist (d. 839).

Maghrib: The Arab West (Northwest Africa).

Mahmud of Ghazna: Turkish Muslim conqueror of India, second ruler of the Ghaznavid dynasty (998–1030).

Mamluk (Mameluke)

al-Ma'mun: Abbasid caliph (813–833); sought to impose Mutazilite kalam vs. piety of men of hadith (q.v.) by *mihna* inquisition.

Mashriq: The Arab East (Arabia and the Fertile Crescent).

Mawali: Arabic (sing. mawla); master or servant; especially in Umayyad times, a non-Arab convert to Islam.

Mecca: City in central Arabia; for Muslims, the holy city to which pilgrimage is made.

Medina: The city in central Arabia to which in A.D. 622 Muhammad and his followers emigrated; the second holiest city for Muslims.

Merv: City in Khurasan (q.v.), in northeastern Iran.

Mudar: A division of the northern (or Qays) bloc of Arab tribes, rivals of Rabi'a (q.v.).

Mufti of Jerusalem: al-Husayni, Hajj Amin (q.v.).

Mughal: Muslim Turkish dynasty which ruled India (1526–1707), also known as Timuri.

Muhammad Iqbal: See Iqbal, Muhammad.

Muqaddasi (also Maqdisi). Muslim geographer (c. 945), author of a valuable description of northwest Africa.

Muradites: Dynasty of Tunisian rulers (1637–1702), under the suzerainty of the Ottoman Empire.

al-Murri, Muslim b. 'Uqba: Commander of Umayyad troops who defeated the Medinese at the battle of al-Harra (q.v.) during the second fitna, or civil war (c. 683).

muruwwa: The moral ethic of pre-Islamic Arabian Bedouin; sometimes called tribal humanism, it included courage, honor, endurance, loyalty, generosity, and hospitality.

Muslim b. 'Uqba al-Murri: See al-Murri, Muslim b. 'Uqba.

mu'tazilism: A school of Islamic thought and kalam (q.v.) stressing human responsibility and divine justice strongly championed by the Abbasid caliph al-Mamun (813–833).

Nahda: The renaissance of Arab culture of the nineteenth and early twentieth centuries.

Nahhas, Mustafa: Egyptian politician, leader of the Wafd party, prime minister (1942–1944).

al-Najaf: Shi'ite holy city in southern Iraq.

Najran: City in northwest Yemen in Arabia.

Neo-Destour Party: See Bourguiba.

Oxus: The Amu Darya, a west-central Asian river.

Qom: Holy city of Twelve-imam Shi'ites in north-central Iran.

Quraysh: Major Meccan clan, from which Muhammad is descended; thereafter, extended family from whom caliph must be selected.

Qutayba b. Muslim: Muslim conqueror of Oxus and Zarafshan basin in central Asia (c. 714).

Rabi'a: Major group within northern (or Qays) bloc of Arab tribes, rivals of Mudar (q.v.).

Rashid al-Kaylani: See al-Jaylani, Rashid Ali.

Rayy: Important Islamic city in pre-Mongol northern Iran.

Safavid: Shi'ite dynasty (1501–1736) which at its height ruled an empire from Iraq to Afghanistan.

Sahnun: Tunisian jurist (c. 800), and author of *Mudawwana*; worked out bases of jurisprudence for Maliki rite.

Sasanid: Persian dynasty (224–642) which ruled an empire that extended from Iraq to Afghanistan; the state religion was Zoroastrianism and the imperial language was Pahlavi.

Sawad: Fertile agricultural province in south-central Iraq, especially important in Abbasid times.

Sayf ibn Umar: Abbasid historian and traditionist (d. 796).

al-Sayyid, Ahmad Lutfi: Prominent Egyptian liberal nationalist journalist (1872–1963), a leader of the People's Party, and editor of *al-Jaridah*.

Sebeos: Armenian bishop, whose *History of Heraclius* is a major source for Byzantine and early Islamic history.

.ul Shariah: Islamic jurisprudence; the discipline of explaining the .ul shariah; also the resultant body of rules.

Shawqi, Ahmad: Modern Egyptian poet (1869–1932), best known for his lyric and romantic poetry.

sikh: Panjabi, disciple; a follower of the syncretistic Hindu faith, Sikhism, founded c. 1500 by Guru Nanak, and having the bulk of its followers in the Panjab, India.

Subki: Author of a *Tabaqat* (c. 900), a collection of biographical notices of Muslims of the Shafi'ite legal rite.

Sufism: Arabic, *tasawwuf*; the commonest term for the Islamic mystical way; some forms of Sufism were heavily influenced by neo-Platonism, others were more scripturalist. An exponent of Sufism is a Sufi.

Sunna: Received custom, particularly that associated with Muhammad; it is embodied in *hadith* (q.v.).

suq: In a Muslim city, the covered market district.

Tabari, Muhammad ibn Jarir al-: Commentator on the Qur'an and historian (839–923), whose *Annals* are the most important historical source on the early Islamic empire.

tafsir: Qur'anic exegesis.

Taftazani: Muslim philosopher-theologian (1322–1389), who wrote numerous works on law, jurisprudence, logic, and metaphysics.

Talaat Pasha: Minister of Interior, later prime minister in Young Turk government (1908–1918).

Tamerlane (Timur-leng): A Chaghatay Turkish general (1336–1405) who established an empire in western and central Asia on the Mongol pattern.

Taqizadeh, Sayyid Hasan: Iranian religious savant and liberal political leader during the Constitutional Revolution (1906–1911).

Thaalbi, Shaykh Abd al-Aziz: Tunisian religious savant and nationalist leader, author of *La Tunisie martyre* (1919).

Savant: specialist in the religious sciences.

Ulama: The traditional teachers of Islam; Muslim scholars.

Umayyad: Islamic dynasty (661–750).

Umma arabiyya: The Arab nation.

Wahhabi: A follower of the Muslim fundamentalist movement founded by Muhammad ibn Abd al-Wahhab (d. 1792), an Arabian preacher and 'alim; one inspired by his teachings.

Yazid I: Umayyad caliph (680–683); his reign was marked by the resumption of civil war among the Arabs.

Zamakhshari, Mahmud al-: Author of a commentary on the Qur'an and an Arabic grammar (1075–1144).

Ziya Gokalp: See Gokalp, Ziya.

# Index

Abbasid dynasty, 44, 92, 110, 115, 122, 131, 135
Abduh, Shaykh Muhammed, 76
Abu Qurra, 10
al-Afghani, Jamal al-Din, 46
Africa, 102, 109, 132
Algeria, 132. *See also* Mahgrib states
Allah, 92
America, 141, 152, 166
Arab countries, 44, 133–142; anti-Semitism of, 78; colonization and, 128, 131–133, 137, 138–139; culture of, 85, 87, 88, 89, 90–94, 115; dialectic in, 139, 140; history of, 135–140; Islam and, 2, 93–94; nationalism of, 31, 37, 56, 126, 128; unitary consciousness of, 34, 126, 137–142; westernization of, 168–173; World War II and, 76–78. *See also* Magian culture; Pseudomorphosis
Arabic language, 44, 135–136, 138
Arabic philosophy, 44
Arabness, 47
Arabs, view of Europe, 4–5, 63
Atatürk, 49, 168
Austria, 75
Averroes, 42, 45, 46, 47
Avicenna, 44, 45, 47

Baathist doctrine, 139
Bacon, Roger, 44, 159
Balzac, Honoré de, 151
Barbarians, 61, 108, 146–147; Islam and, 109–110
Bash Hamba, Ali, 79
Becker, C. H., 54, 59–60, 168
Bedouins, 47, 54, 63
Béguin, Albert, 33
Bergson, Henri, 36, 176 n. 19
Bismarck, Otto von, 75
Boulainvilliers, Henri de, 22, 28, 35
Buddhism, 66, 67, 71, 72
Byzantine empire, 10, 109, 112, 135

*Chanson de Roland*, 12
Chateaubriand, 29, 176 n. 12
China, 2, 4, 36, 104, 107, 109, 111, 112–113, 123; civilizing impulse of, 108; Islam and, 109
Christendom, 10–11, 74, 109
Christianity, 10, 13, 19, 48, 58–60, 66, 69, 71, 86, 91, 104, 143, 159; in France, 159–160; Islam's challenge and, 15–16, 17, 159
Civilization. *See* European civilization; Islamic civilization
Counter-Reformation, 159, 160
Crusades, 10–12, 35, 70, 109

195

Designer: UC Press Staff
Compositor: Trend Western
Printer: Braun-Brumfield, Inc.
Binder: Braun-Brumfield, Inc.
Text: 9/13 Palatino
Display: Palatino